T0337539

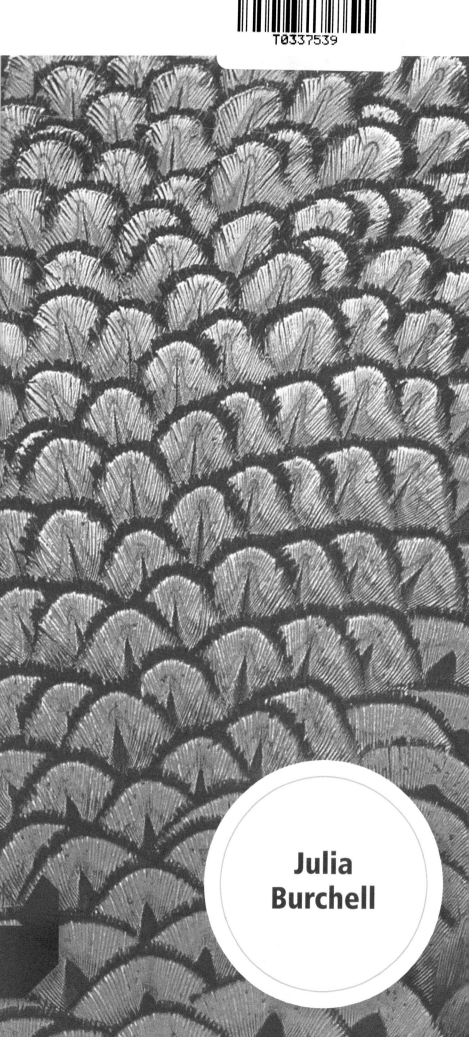

CAMBRIDGE IGCSE® ENGLISH

Revision Guide

Julia Burchell

ACKNOWLEDGEMENTS

Published by Letts Educational
An imprint of HarperCollins*Publishers*
The News Building
1 London Bridge Street
London
SE1 9GF

HarperCollins*Publishers* Ltd
Macken House
39/40 Mayor Street Upper
Dublin 1
D01 C9W8
Ireland

ISBN 9780008210366

First published 2018

10 9 8 7

© HarperCollins*Publishers* Limited 2018

® IGCSE is a registered trademark.
All exam-style questions, related example answers, marks awarded and comments that appear in this book were written
by the author. In examinations, the way marks would be awarded to questions and answers like these may be different.

Julia Burchell asserts her moral right to be identified as the author of this work.

All rights reserved. No part of this publication may be reproduced, stored in a retrieval system, or transmitted in any form
or by any means, electronic, photocopying, recording or otherwise, without the prior written
permission of Letts Educational.

British Library Cataloguing in Publication Data
A CIP record for this book is available from the British Library.

Commissioned by Gillian Bowman
Project managed by Rachel Allegro
Edited by Jill Laidlaw
Proofread by Sam Lacey and Louise Robb
Cover design by Paul Oates
Typesetting by QBS
Production by Natalia Rebow and Lyndsey Rogers
Printed and bound in the UK by Ashford Colour Press Ltd.

Whilst every effort has been made to trace the copyright holders, in cases where this has been unsuccessful, or if any have
inadvertently been overlooked, the Publishers would gladly receive any information enabling them to rectify any error or
omission at the first opportunity.

Cover and p.1: © Worraket / Shutterstock; p.8: © 2016 The Scientist; p.12: Reproduced with permission. Copyright © (2013)
Scientific American, a division of Nature America, Inc. All rights reserved.; p.20: © 2015 The Telegraph; p.56: © The Week /
Dennis Publishing Ltd 2016; p.72 & 73: Excerpts from THE WATER'S LOVELY by Ruth Rendell, copyright © 2006 by Kings-
markham Enterprises, Ltd.. Used by permission of Crown Publishing Group, and
Hutchinson, divisions of Penguin Random House LLC. All rights reserved.

MIX
Paper | Supporting
responsible forestry
FSC™ C007454
www.fsc.org

This book contains FSC™ certified paper and other controlled
sources to ensure responsible forest management.

For more information visit: www.harpercollins.co.uk/green

Contents

Section 1: Reading

Section 2: Directed writing and composition

This revision guide is designed to support your studies for Cambridge IGCSE and IGCSE (9–1) First Language English. It contains content linked to the syllabus, highlights key strategies and approaches, provides revision tips, and suggests activities and questions you might like to work through in order to prepare for the examination.

However, it is important to remember that this is a revision guide. It covers all of the syllabus content but it does not contain the depth and detail you might get from your own notes or from a textbook. It is therefore a good idea to use this book as one of the tools to help you prepare for examination but it should not necessarily be the only tool in your toolkit.

The focus of this revision guide is the skills needed for Papers 1 and 2. All students do Paper 1, but you will need to talk to your teacher about whether you will be doing Paper 2 – it depends whether you are taking the coursework or written paper option.

The content is arranged into two sections.

- Section 1 is about the skills for Paper 1 and is divided up into four chapters: comprehension questions, summary writing questions, short answer and language questions, and writing questions. At the end of each topic area you will find an exam-style task.
- Section 2 covers preparations for Paper 2 and is organised into three chapters: directed writing questions, composition questions – description, and composition questions – narrative.

When you look at the topic areas you will notice that some words are in bold. These are key terms you will need to learn and be able to use. The definitions for these words can be found in the Glossary at the back of the book, which is arranged in topic areas. This means that it should be fairly straightforward to find the meanings of the key words that you need.

Each topic area takes you step by step through some of the key approaches to the focus task, or breaks down the elements of a good answer.

Revision tips appear in each topic area. These might suggest a framework to make approaches to questions easier to remember or they may highlight particular concepts that students typically get confused about. Each topic area also has a number of activities for you to have a go at. You may want to approach these in a variety of ways. For example, if you are confident with the content, you might want to try some of the activities without using your notes and against the clock. However, if there are parts of the syllabus you are struggling to understand or which are difficult to learn, you could use your notes and textbook to complete the activities. Answers for the activities are provided at the back of the book. The activities, questions, example answers, marks awarded and comments that appear in the book were written by the author. Note that in examinations, the way marks would be awarded to answers like these may be different.

Finally, have a think about how you revise. While you may want to focus on your own learning, it is always a good idea to meet up with other students and, for at least some of the time, revise together. Try battling against the clock and each other to find summary points or answer short questions. With the longer tasks, you can help each other with aspects one of you might not understand and make comments about each other's work to help improve it. Most importantly, revision with someone else is usually more fun and productive than when you revise on your own.

Understanding comprehension questions

You must be able to:

- Understand what comprehension questions are
- Understand what is required to answer a comprehension question.

What types of comprehension question are there?

There are two different types of comprehension question:

- questions that test your ability to understand explicit information (E)
- questions that test your ability to understand implicit information (I)

> **Revision tip**

Go over some sample questions and code the questions (E) or (I) to build your confidence when approaching the comprehension section.

SKILLS BUILDER 1

> Look at the questions below. Decide which type of question each one is. (You do not have the article that these questions refer to at this point, as your focus is on the question types, not finding answers.)

1. Using your own words explain what the writer meant by: 'the result seems very robust'.

2. Explain what scientists used to believe was the cause of the decline of dinosaurs on Earth.

3. Identify the evidence which was used as the basis of the new theory.

4. Using your own words explain what the text means by:
   (i) 'already past their prime'
   (ii) 'under stress'

5. Give two reasons why scientists believe that dinosaurs died out on Earth.

6. Explain what the writer meant by 'some kind of long death march'.

What forms of comprehension question are there?

There are several different forms of comprehension question.

- Questions which ask you to 'give' or identify things found in the text.
- Questions which ask you what the writer 'says' or has written about something.
- Questions which ask you to explain in your own words.

SKILLS BUILDER 2

> Go back over the six sample questions given earlier and identify which form of question they are.

Which skills do you need to answer comprehension questions?

It is important not to misinterpret the type of question being asked or you may end up copying out a piece of information when the question tests your ability to explain, or writing about explicit meaning when the question is testing **inferences**.

You need to focus in on the command words in the question, in order to be sure about what you should be doing.

Look at this table, which gives the command words, the skills they signal you to use, and the type of question they usually appear in.

Command word	What you need to do	Type of question
Give/Identify	Find a word or phrase and write it down.	Explicit meaning questions
Explain using your own words what the text means by (then gives you a word or phrase)	'Translate' specific words that the writer has written to show that you understood the literal meaning.	Translation questions
Explain…	Requires you to use explicit and/or implicit understanding to give reasoning for a viewpoint or idea.	Reasoning questions

SKILLS BUILDER 3

Highlight the command words in the questions at the start of this unit.

Answering short answer questions

You must be able to:

- Understand how to locate the relevant words or phrases to answer short answer comprehension questions
- Learn how to explain what writers mean by the words and phrases that they use.

How to locate key words and phrases

Often the question will tell you a paragraph or line number to help you to locate the answer. As you read each question circle any such information.

SKILLS BUILDER 4

Read the text below from the-scientist.com, and then alter the questions on the next page so that they give a clear indication of where to look for the answer. The first two have been completed for you.

A giant asteroid slammed into the Earth in the area of today's Yucutan Peninsula 66 million years ago. The dramatic event has, for decades, been posited as the reason that many dinosaurs—along with scores of other fossil species—went extinct. But at least for dinosaurs, that galactic catastrophe may have been less of an instantaneous apocalypse and more of a final death blow to species already in slow and steady decline, according to a study published in PNAS yesterday (April 18). In it, researchers in the U.K. proposed that many dinosaur species were in pretty bad shape for at least 48 million years prior to the asteroid's impact.

"One of the things that has been long debated about dinosaur evolution is whether they were reigning strong right up until the time of the meteorite impact, or whether there was a slow, gradual decrease in [the emergence of new species] or an increase in extinction before that time," study coauthor Chris Venditti, an evolutionary biologist at the University of Reading, told The Guardian.

"We were not expecting this result," said study coauthor Manabu Sakamoto, also of Reading, in a statement. "While the asteroid impact is still the prime candidate for the dinosaurs' final disappearance, it is clear that they were already past their prime in an evolutionary sense."

Sakamoto, Venditti, and University of Bristol paleontologist Michael Benton modeled the rates of dinosaur speciation events and found that new species were not arising as quickly as old ones went extinct for millions of years of dinosaur evolution. "I think that dinosaurs were probably under stress for a very long time," Sakomoto told The Atlantic.

Meantime, other recent paleontological models posited that dinosaur species were doing just fine when the huge meteorite struck the Earth. In a Biological Reviews paper published last year, University of Edinburgh paleontologist Stephen Brusatte and colleagues suggested that there was "no evidence for a progressive decline in total dinosaur species richness."

"I love seeing big datasets and new methods thrown at some of these classic mysteries," Brusatte, speaking of the new PNAS paper, told The Atlantic. "The result seems very robust, but I question what it means. Does that mean that dinosaurs were doomed to extinction, that they endured some kind of long death march before the asteroid impact finished them off, like a boxer knocking down their opponent with a light punch after several rounds of pummeling? I don't think so."

1. Using your own words explain what the writer meant by: 'the result seems very robust'. (Paragraph 6)

2. Explain what scientists used to believe was the cause of the decline of dinosaurs on earth. (line 1)

3. Identify the evidence which was used as the basis of the new theory.

4. Using your own words explain what the text means by:

    (i) 'already past their prime'

    (ii) 'under stress'

5. Give two reasons why scientists believe that dinosaurs died out on Earth.

6. Explain what the writer meant by 'some kind of long death march'.

How to write up your answer

State/What

When a question asks you to 'give' in your answer, or asks you to 'identify' then you should simply give the exact word or phrase from the text without writing it into a sentence or copying out unnecessary words.

For example, Question 3 above asked: Identify the evidence which was used as the basis of the new theory.

You would find your answer in the paragraph: "Sakamoto, Venditti, and University of Bristol paleontologist Michael Benton modelled the rates of dinosaur speciation events and found that new species were not arising as quickly as old ones went extinct for millions of years of dinosaur evolution. "I think that dinosaurs were probably under stress for a very long time," Sakomoto told The Atlantic.

However, you do not need all of this information.

Your answer could be: 'Benton's models of dinosaur speciation events.'

Explain in your own words

If a question asks you to 'explain in your own words' then it is important not to re-use words from the text as the question is testing whether or not you have understood the original words; you need to prove that you have understood by translating them.

For example, Question 1 asks: 'Using your own words explain what the writer meant by: 'the result seems very robust'.

Ask yourself what word you could use instead of 'robust'. Make sure that the synonym that you choose matches 'robust' precisely. So, whilst you could pick 'good', this would not suggest strength, which the original word does.

A good answer would be: Very strong and stands up to attack.

Now answer questions 1–6 using the text and your altered questions from skills builder 4.

Answering questions which require inference

You must be able to:

- Understand that writers encourage us to think about their ideas by deliberately choosing words which lead us to 'read between the lines' and to draw conclusions (or inferences)
- Explain inferences that words have led you to and why.

Working out inferences from words

You will usually be given specific words or phrases to consider.

- If they are about people then you will usually be looking for hints about feelings (F), attitudes (A) or relationships (R).
- If they are about places then you will usually be looking for a sense of atmosphere (A).

You need to look at the words selected for you to consider; firstly, work out what they mean literally and then what this suggests.

For example, read this extract from a passage about the reactions of scientists to the new theory about dinosaurs.

'Scientists are gritting their teeth as they await the storm of criticism which will surely follow new revelations about the extinction of the dinosaurs.'

Now look at how the literal and then implicit meanings can be unpicked.

gritting their teeth

MEANS – they are clenching their teeth together

SUGGESTS – they don't feel happy/perhaps in pain/holding back emotion/words?

Your answer could be:

I have learned that they are not happy, and may be uncomfortable about the findings and have their own ideas about them that they are trying not to say.

Revision tip

Remember these four foci by using F A R A as a checklist.

Read the following paragraph, which describes the scientists' reactions further.

When we asked for opinions on the new theory, the scientists from The Institute shift in their seats and several begin to tap repeatedly with their pens and laser pointers. 'The thing is..' one begins and then halts, looking quickly around the room, 'we have to consider a lot of other evidence; the destruction of numerous species; not just the dinosaurs.' Another colleague nodded quickly and then sat upright again. 'It is not popular to disagree with the new ideas but I find it difficult to agree', he told us. The debate will no doubt continue but these scientists seem certain that the new theory is not one to waste too much time and attention on.

What can you infer about the scientists from the highlighted words and phrases? Create four flow charts to show your thinking.

Writing about inferences

You will not need to write very much but it helps you to keep focused if you start your answer by using part of the question stem.

For example, if a question asked: What do you learn about the scientists from the word 'nodded quickly' in the final paragraph?

Your answer might be:

I have learned that the scientists agree but are anxious about showing their views.

Revision tip

Be careful not to write too much and waste time on this type of question. If you are expected to explain the words chosen in detail, then there will be a larger space for writing and more marks available.

Answer this question.
What do you learn about the scientist from '…but I find it difficult to agree' at the end of the paragraph?

Read the extract below taken from scientificamerican.com

Then answer the exam-style questions below.

Extinct Species That People Still Hope to Rediscover

There's nothing like the scientific thrill of discovering something for the very first time—or, in rare cases, rediscovering something that most people had presumed forever lost. Take the Cuban solenodon (*Solenodon cubanus*), for example. Unseen after 1890 and long presumed extinct, it unexpectedly showed up again in 1974. Sightings after that were few and far between but scientists kept looking. Last year, after a 10-year search, an international team led by Rafael Borroto-Páez rediscovered the solenodon in a remote mountain park, a finding that thrilled scientists on both sides of the globe.

Unfortunately, most similar quests to find presumed-extinct species don't have such happy endings. In some cases the lost creatures are rediscovered, but even in those rare cases the findings usually come barely in time: Only a few dozen members of the species remain, tucked into tiny habitats facing increasing pressures from encroaching civilization. More often than not the quests remain quixotic: endless, lonely and fruitless. That doesn't stop the scientists or other explorers. Sometimes they keep hunting for decades, looking in every odd corner they can reach, keening at every step for success.

1. The Thylacine, or Tasmanian Tiger (*Thylacinus cynocephalus*)

The last known Thylacine died in Hobart Zoo in Tasmania in 1936 after decades of needless persecution by farmers who mistakenly thought the wide-jawed beasts would kill off their sheep. Today, nearly 80 years after the last Thylacine passed away, people still search the remote wilds of Tasmania for signs that it might still exist. An Australian magazine even offered a $1.25-million bounty for proof that the species still lived in remote regions, and a Tasmanian businessman offered a $1.8-million reward. Hundreds of people have gone looking, and bits and pieces of "evidence" have turned up from time to time. Most recently two brothers came across a strange skull that they claimed had to have come from a Thylacine. No such luck: it turned out to be a dog skull.

The quest for the Thylacine is so powerful and so emotional that it has made its way into fiction several times recently, most notably in the 2001 novel *The Hunter* by Julia Leigh, which was adapted in 2011 into an excellent film starring Willem Dafoe. Much less effective was the awful 2008 horror film *Dying Breed* starring Saw screenwriter and actor, Leigh Whannell. The Tasmanian tiger deserved better.

1 Give an example of a rediscovered 'extinct' species according to the text.

.... [1]

2 Using your own words, explain what the text means by:

(i) presumed forever lost (line 2)

....

.... [2]

(ii) needless persecution (lines 15–16)

....

.... [2]

(iii) remote regions (line 19)

....

.... [2]

3 Re-read paragraph 2

Give two reasons why most searches for extinct species end sadly.

....

.... [2]

4 Re-read paragraphs 3 and 4

(i) Identify two pieces of evidence to show that re-discovering is an appealing idea to many people.

....

.... [2]

5 Using your own words explain how the writer felt when he wrote 'No such luck'. (Line 24)

....

.... [2]

6 Explain why people want to re-discover a 'lost' species?

....

.... [2]

Understanding summary questions

You must be able to:

- Understand what summary questions are
- Understand what is usually needed to answer a summary question.

What is a summary question?

A summary question asks you to read a passage and then pick out a set number of **main ideas** and then rewrite the passage in a more concise way (which means you should not give examples or details) according to that specific focus. The question usually sets a word limit for your answer.

The following question refers to a **Passage B**, which is about paragliding. (You do not have a copy of the passage as this task is about looking closely at the question *not* answering it.) Look at the question and the annotations. The annotations show how you should use each part of the instructions.

3   *This tells you how to write the second part of your answer.*

According to Text B what is paragliding like and what are the writer's thoughts and feelings about it?

This tells you what to write about.

This tells you how to write up your answer.

You must use continuous writing (not note form) and use your own words as far as possible.

This tells you how much to write.

Your summary in question **3 (a)** must be no more than 150 words.

10 marks are available for the content of your answer and up to 5 marks are available for the quality of your writing.

This tells you how your work will be marked.

> ### Revision tip
>
> Practice finding synonyms for words as you come across them in everyday life. This will broaden your vocabulary for the exam.

Write your own summary question, making sure that your instructions contain all of the important elements shown above.

What skills do you need to use to answer a summary question?

The question on these pages uses a blend of reading and writing skills and also uses different skills – note-making when you are preparing to write a written summary.

Preparation

- Read the question carefully and identify the focus of the task.
- **Scan** to find the details needed.
- Understand **literal** and **implicit** meanings in the passage.
- Select so that only the relevant information is used for your notes.

Written summary

- Use **synonyms** and **paraphrasing** to ensure that your own words are used in the written summary.
- Select so that the answer is concise and is written to a word limit.

Preparing for summary questions

You must be able to:

- Scan and select relevant ideas from a text
- Copy these ideas down so that they answer the question that has been set.

How to scan for relevant ideas in a text

The summary question will give you a focus for your scanning. The focus is on the main ideas of a passage not the examples and details given. You need to 'sieve out' what is needed and leave the rest.

Follow these three steps to make sure that your focus is accurate.

- **Step one:** Find the question focus to create the start of a sentence, e.g. if the summary question says: What do you learn from the passage about the dangers of rock climbing?

- **Step two:** Then use this to make a sentence starter which you keep in mind, e.g. One danger of rock climbing is …

- **Step three:** Read each sentence of the passage and see if you can use them to complete your sentence by interrogating them.

For example, a piece of text that explores a group's experiences caving in Iceland has the following summary question:

> What preparations have to be made before an ice-caving expedition?

Step one: The summary question asks me to focus on the preparation needed before going ice-caving.

Step two: My sentence starter will be: Before going ice-caving you need to …

Step three: I will read the relevant sentence – 'My friends and I decided at quite short notice to take a trip out to Svínafellsjökull but were really disappointed when we got there as all the tours were fully booked, and had been for months.'

I will interrogate the sentence:

Does this tell me a preparation that they made?   **No**

Can I infer that a preparation was made?   **No**

Do I learn anything about preparations at all?   **Yes** – they didn't make any preparations and so they missed out. They should have booked early.

Interrogate the paragraph below using **step one** and **step two** from the example above, which answers the following question:

What preparations have to be made before an ice-caving expedition?

The ice cave season in Iceland is rather short or from November to March. Outside of that season it can be dangerous to go into the caves because they can collapse, which is, well, dangerous. I'm guessing the reason is that it's not cold enough. So if a visit to an ice cave is on the top of your Iceland bucket list, the window is small.

Make sure you use main ideas only

It is important not to include examples and detail in a summary. To do this you need to be confident about what these types of information are so that you can avoid them, for example:

'All necessary glacier gear is included, including crampons and helmet.'

Main idea   examples

> **Revision tip**

You do not always have to use a synonym in a summary as some words are not easy to replace.

Identify the main ideas and examples or detail in the sentence below.

Clothing was the next thing to get right before I left! You have to wear layers, microfibre is best: vest, sweater and fleece plus gloves and only the foolish forget thermal underwear!

Make sure you write your notes clearly so that they are useable

Your notes must be clear and concise but they must also still be an obvious idea that fits the summary focus.

Look at the following notes, each one made in response to this question:

Summarise the health issues that can affect mountain climbers.

Use this sentence:

Danger is at every corner – rope burns from pulleys, kit webbing and hand rails are omnipresent.

(a) Skin grazes

(b) Friction burns

(c) Mountain climbers can get friction rubs from the ropes they use.

Note **(c)** is too long. Note **(a)** is very general and does not cover the idea that the injuries are from ropes rubbing as the student has tried to find a synonym when there is not a precise enough one available for rope burns. Note **(b)** is short and precise.

Writing in summary style

You must be able to:

- Order points logically
- Write in summary style (be concise/be objective/use your own words).

How to order the points you make

You will need to find at least ten points in your notes but it is not advisable to copy them out just as you have listed them, as the list is likely to represent the order that they appeared in the passage rather than have any other logic.

Instead, ask yourself whether you can group the ten points in any way. For instance, look at this set of notes made in answer to the following question about 'tomb-stoners' – people who jump off cliffs into the water below.

> What tips are given to help tomb-stoners avoid injury?

1. Check the depth of the water beforehand
2. Keep body straight when diving
3. Check that cliff edge is secure
4. Make sure other divers are on look out
5. Make sure lifeguards are on look out
6. Make sure no rocks in water
7. Wear goggles when diving
8. Avoid sites with record of injuries
9. Check for riptides or strong currents
10. Wear a knife

These could be grouped into a simple order: Before the dive and during the dive.

SKILLS BUILDER 4

> Can you think of any other ways of grouping the points above?

Write in a summary style

There are several important things to remember about summary style.

1. Things to leave out

- Do not give opinions.
- Do not add comments / introductions / conclusions.
- Do not add detail or examples.

SKILLS BUILDER 5

Look at this example of a summary written using the notes about tomb-stoning. Even though this summary covers all of the points, it is not a good answer as it is not in the correct style. As you read, annotate it (O) for opinions, (C) for comments, (D) for detail and (E) for examples.

I am going to write about advice to give tomb-stoners. I think tomb-stoners are mad but if they're going to do it then I think the least they can do is to check the alluring cliffs online first and see if they have a bad safety record; either injuries, cliff erosions or sea issues. The thing is, if they don't wear a knife and goggles then they can't cut themselves free of any rope or weeds they might land in, if there is any trouble (which is stupid) and if they haven't booked lifeguards or friends to keep a lookout then they're really on their own if they've got injured by hitting rocks or the bottom. This would be my advice.

2. Things to include

- A clear topic sentence, which links your comments to the passage and to the focus of the question, e.g. Passage A gives several tips to tomb-stoners, to help them avoid injury.
- Complex sentences that use commas, colons and semicolons to outline linked ideas, rather than adding extra words by repeating sentence starters, e.g. Some tips are about preparations that tomb-stoners should complete such as checking the record of the proposed jump site; making sure there are no rocks, tidal problems or cliff erosion and organising lifeguards or attendants to be there.

Exam-style practice questions

Read carefully **Passage B, The daredevils attempting the "climb of the century"**, in the Reading Booklet and then answer Question 1.

Passage B

The daredevils attempting the "climb of the century"

Just how difficult is it to scale the Dawn Wall of El Capitan, the 3,000 ft rock face in Yosemite National Park, California? Not to drill bolts into its sheer, smooth, granite and heave yourself up with ropes, but to free climb, using nothing but steely fingers and rubber-soled climbing shoes, with a harness only to prevent catastrophe in case of a fall. The climbers Tommy Caldwell and Kevin Jorgeson are finding out right now, in an attempt that has gripped the world, as the pair tweet and use social media to broadcast live updates of their progress. Not since hardy Bavarians set out to conquer the north face of the Eiger in the 1930s have climbers so publicly defied death. Then, an audience looked on from the comfort of chalets at the foot of the mountain; today, spectators look up agog from Yosemite's valley floor or keep track around the world on their mobile phones.

Caldwell and Jorgeson have split the immense Dawn Wall into 32 "pitches", or sections, of varying length and difficulty. On pitch 16 of their route, which has taken them seven years to map and devise, there is what is known in the mountaineering game as a "dyno", or dynamic manoeuvre. It requires the climber to jump six feet horizontally, then seize hold of a minuscule rock edge, which actually slopes downwards, in the hope that this pitiful handhold will prevent their momentum from carrying them off the granite and into the void. It is a move from the fevered imaginations of Hollywood screenwriters, who employed something similar in the opening credits of *Mission: Impossible 2*, starring Tom Cruise. Except that Caldwell and Jorgeson do not benefit from special effects.

But pitch 16 is not the hardest pitch of the ascent. With its devilishly demanding combination of handholds and footholds, pitch 14 is. That's how hard it is to climb the Dawn Wall. Rock climbers grade ascents using numbers, from 5.0 to 5.15. Steep ascents with good holds are rated 5.0–5.4. The hand and footholds at the upper end can be literally razor-blade thin, so that climbers slice open their fingers as they cling to the face. Pitch 16, with its almost absurd "dyno", is rated 5.13 (or, as one outdoors website puts it: "If you can climb upside down on a glass window, these climbs are right up your alley"). Pitches 14 and 15 are both rated one notch higher, at 5.14.

Although Caldwell first conceived the idea of free climbing the Dawn Wall in 2007 (he was joined in the venture by Jorgeson, the less experienced climber, in 2009), it was not until 2013 that he managed to free climb pitch 15. And finally, last November, Caldwell completed the dreaded pitch 14, leaving the pair ready to put their years of practice and research to good use and tick off one pitch after another in a single expedition, thus becoming the first men to free climb the entire Dawn Wall in one go. Caldwell has done 12 practice free climbs on El Capitan. For Jorgeson, this is the first.

The daredevils attempting the "climb of the century", *The Week*, 17 Jan. 2015

1 According to text B, what were the challenges facing Jorgeson and Caldwell?

You must use continuous writing (not note form) and use your own words as far as possible. Your summary should not be more than 150 words. Up to 10 marks are available for the content of your answer and 5 marks are available for the quality of your writing.

....

....

....

....

....

....

....

....

....

....

....

....

....

....

....

....

....

....   [15]

Understanding short answer and language questions

You must be able to:

- Understand what short answer and language questions are
- Understand the key concepts and skills that are used to answer these questions.

What are short answer and language questions?

Short answer and language questions are always based on an unseen passage that you will be asked to read.

Short answer and language questions may appear in a few different question forms. Here are some examples of typical questions and the key concepts and skills that they require you to use are outlined below each of them. Key concepts are in italics.

Question form a)

> Identify a word or phrase which suggests the same idea as the words underlined.

This form of question is testing your literal understanding of the passage. You will need to *understand the literal meaning* of the words or phrases you have been given and then *scan* for a word or phrase from the passage and copy it out.

Question form b)

> Using your own words, explain what the writer means by each of the words underlined.

This form of question is testing your literal understanding of the passage. You will need to *understand the literal meaning* of the words you have been given.

Question form c)

> Using your own words, explain how the phrases underlined are used by the writer to suggest xxxx

This form of question identifies phrases from the passage and tells you what they suggest. (This could be a specific effect such as an idea or emotion, or a **sensory picture**, or an emotional reaction it provokes.) You are asked to *explain* how the words achieve the *effect*. To do this you need to use your *understanding of the literal meanings* of words, the *implicit meanings of words* and the way that writers use *language devices*.

Question form d)

> Re-read the descriptions of:
>
> X
>
> and
>
> x
>
> Select four powerful words or phrases from each paragraph. Your choices should include imagery. Explain how each word or phrase selected is used effectively in the context. Write about 200–300 words.

This form of question is known as a Language Question and combines all of the skills you have used in the other forms of question and also adds the extra skill of being able to select *'powerful'* words or phrases for yourself.

SKILLS BUILDER 1

Go over a set of exam-style or past-paper questions. Annotate them with the key skills that you will need to use in order to answer them.

Showing that you understand literal meanings

You must be able to:
- Understand literal meanings
- Scan passages for synonyms.

Showing that you understand literal meanings

Question forms a) and b) from 'Understanding short answer and language questions' both test your literal understanding of what you have read.

Form a) offers you a translation of the original word and then asks you to find the original. You need to break this process into three steps:

1. Think of synonyms for the word/s you have been given.

2. Scan the passage looking for the moment they are used.

3. Identify the synonym and copy it out.

Read the following exemplar question:

<u>Sentence given</u>: Sandeep wanted the birthday gift to be <u>the only one of its kind</u>.

<u>Passage</u>:

It was his Mother's first birthday since he had been working. It was never a special day for her and the gifts she received were so predictable; a new diary, some cosmetics, a paperback and of course…chocolates. He wanted to show her how much thought he had put into her day. The day must be a special one for her and his gift must be unique to reflect his new job and status in the community.

Now look at a student's notes which answer it by following the steps:

Step one: synonyms – rare / unusual / unique

Step two: scan looking for the word gift or present – this will locate the rough area of the synonym.

Step three: identify the synonym and copy it out – unique.

> Now complete steps 1–3 using these new exemplar questions and the passage above.
> Sentence given: His mother always got the <u>same</u> type of presents.
> Sentence given: He wanted the day to be <u>less routine and mundane</u>.

Form b) gives you a word from a passage and asks you to explain it in your own words. This is quite straightforward as long as you find an explanation which expresses the precise meaning of the words in the text. This can be achieved in two steps:

1. Re-read the whole sentence making sure you are clear exactly what the underlined word adds to it.

2. Think of a number of synonyms.

3. Then use several so that your explanation includes all of the associations and nuances needed.

Read the following exemplar question.

Using your own words, explain what the writer means by each of the underlined words or phrases:

He awoke early on her Birthday and leapt out of bed, springing <u>enthusiastically as if to attention. (1)</u> The sun was shining brightly and he smiled, accepting it as an omen for the party he had planned with military <u>meticulousness. (2)</u> Firstly he needed to get to the bakery to collect the cake he had ordered. It was iced in her favourite colours, and had two model birds on the top; hummingbirds – blue and green – he had rigidly <u>dictated (3)</u> his wishes clearly over the phone. He would not be happy if they had not delivered his wishes exactly.

Now look at a student's notes which answer it by following the steps.

Step one: The word is about how he feels and acts – it describes his state of being.

Step two: with interest / with energy / with passion / gusto / zeal / positive

Final answer:

It means that he got up with a great deal of energy and positivity about what he was planning to do.

> Now complete steps 1–3 using the two remaining underlined words in the exemplar question and the passage above.

Revision tip

Remember that many words come with **implicit** meanings / associations; positive and negative or unconscious links to other concepts. These all need to be explained as well as the literal meaning of a word.

SKILLS BUILDER 3

Showing that you understand implicit meanings

You must be able to:

- Explain how phrases have implicit meanings.

Explaining implicit meanings

Question form c) tests whether you can explain what is suggested by phrases – that is, the implications they suggest.

However a c) form question will tell you the phrases to explain so your job is only to explain *what suggestions the phrases create.*

Read the following exemplar question which uses the passage you studied in 'Showing that you understand literal meanings'.

Using your own words, explain how the phrases underlined are used by the writer to suggest Prakesh's personality and feelings.

He awoke early on her birthday and leapt out of bed, <u>springing up enthusiastically as if to attention. (1)</u> The sun was shining brightly and he smiled, accepting it as an omen for the party he had planned with <u>military meticulousness. (2)</u> Firstly he needed to get to the bakery to collect the cake he had ordered. It was iced in her favourite colours, and had two model birds on the top; hummingbirds – blue and green – he had <u>rigidly dictated (3)</u> his wishes clearly over the phone. He would not be happy if they had not delivered his wishes exactly.

Now look at a student's notes which they made whilst preparing to answer it.

Phrase	Implicit meaning/associations
springing up enthusiastically as if to attention	'springing' suggests he gets up instantly – very motivated. 'attention' makes me think of the military – makes me wonder if he is very organised and follows a routine?

Complete a table like the one above for the other two phrases in the exemplar task above.

It would be easy to write at length about your notes, but you need to be guided by the space that you have been allowed for writing your answer and also the number of marks available. This suggests that your answer should only be a sentence or two long.

Here is the answer given by the student whose notes you saw above:

He is very motivated and perhaps is quite organised and likes a routine.

Revision tip

Remember not to waste time repeating the question stem or writing an introduction for this question.

Understanding language questions

You must be able to:

- Understand what language questions are
- Understand the skills used to answer a language question.

What is a language question?

Language questions often have a familar wording and layout. Here is an example of a typical question, with the key features labelled 1–5.

Re-read the descriptions (1) of:

(a) the boat in paragraph 5

(b) the harbour in paragraph 3.

Select four powerful words and phrases from each paragraph. (2) Your choices should include imagery. (3) Explain how each word or phrase selected is used effectively in the context. (3)

Write about 200–300 words. (4)

Up to 15 marks are available for the content of your answer. (5)

If you read the question carefully, you may be able to work out:

1. Where to look for the pieces of text that your answer will be based on.
2. How many words to select.
3. What to include in your answer.
4. How much to write.
5. How your work will be assessed.

SKILLS BUILDER 5

Write **three** sample questions of your own and annotate them with the **five** features outlined above. This will help you to understand what this type of question includes.

Skills that may help you to approach language questions:
A Understand what 'powerful words' means

The most fundamental skill that you need is to understand what a powerful word or phrase is. This will help you to select the words to focus on in your answer.

When a writer puts pen to paper they are hoping to affect you in some way.

If they do, then this is called a writer's effect.

Read the following comments made by four students after reading the same paragraph.

Revision tip

When answering a writer's effect question, remember LISDE (Literal, Implicit, Sensory, Devices, Effect).

A. Wow! That was so exciting . . . it took my breath away!

B. Oh that poor man, he was so scared and upset.

C. I can just picture that house after the wrecking ball hit it; smashed to bits!

D. I'm never, ever going to forget that. I couldn't stop reading.

Match the speech bubbles to the writer's effects below.

1. To gain and keep attention	2. To provoke a reaction	3. To convey an idea, attitude, emotion or mood	4. To create a sensory picture

Where words create an effect these can be described as powerful.

These are the words and phrases you need to pick out to write about in a language question.

SKILLS BUILDER 6

Look at the sentence below. How does the sentence demonstrate each of the effects listed above?

The boy clawed at the door, shredding the painted wood so that it lay in vicious splinters on the ground under him as he whined in despair.

Skills that may help you to approach language questions:
B Understand how effects are created

The next skill you need is to be able to explain *how* those effects were created. There are several ways of doing this.

- Explain the literal meaning of the words used.
- Explain the implicit meanings created by the words used.
- Explain the sensory images the words create.
- Explain the language devices that are used.

Identifying an effect and selecting the words which show it

You must be able to:
- Understand what an effect is
- Select the exact word/s which create an effect.

What is a writer's effect?

All writers want to **engage** you in what they have written. They may want you to *understand and react* to their ideas and feelings and they may want you to be able to *imagine the people and places* they describe and *feel emotions* about them. These are writer's effects.

There are several different types of effect:

- An effect which captures and keeps your attention.

- An effect which conveys a specific meaning / attitude / viewpoint / mood / emotion.

- An effect which creates a sensory picture in the reader's mind.

- An effect which provokes a specific emotion.

SKILLS BUILDER 7

Read this extract from an account of a business trip to Ulaanbaatar, the capital city of Mongolia. Then decide which of the statements below best sum up the effect the text had on you.

I was as outside my comfort zone as I had ever been. Not because the welcome wasn't warm, or the work interesting, but because there was nothing, nothing at all, that was familiar or easy or comfortable about it. From the tentative, shuffling steps that I would take on the packed, deep, ice-clad pavements, to the crisp spikiness of my own eyelashes, scraping the balaclava which clung damply to my ruby-red, rigid cheeks – everything was alien.

- I was drawn to this passage and want to read on.

- I can really understand how the writer felt about their trip and why.

- I can picture and 'feel' what the writer saw and felt.

- I now have strong feelings about Ulaanbaatar.

How to select effective words

The key to recognising (and then selecting) an effect is to read a text slowly and carefully whilst interrogating it. The easiest way to do this is to keep a checklist in your mind and draw a conclusion at the end of each sentence.

Here is a possible checklist.

- Is there something jumping out and catching my attention?
- Am I getting a strong message?
- Am I imagining that I am there?
- Am I feeling anything?

Revision tip

You can remember this checklist by using AMIF as an aide de memoir. It is made up of the initial letters of key words: A (attention), M (message), I (imagining), F (feeling).

Complete the table showing how the paragraph below could be interrogated, step by step.

SKILLS BUILDER 8

> The horizon was a puzzle; the jarring silhouettes of grey concrete blocks of flats, flanked by squat, smoking clusters of yurts and distant mountain ranges made no sense to my eye. As each expelled their workers into the city; some in smart suits and winter coats, others in their national costume of a thick padded Del, broad corset like sashes, 'hoof' sleeves and boots with upturned toes, I was fascinated and unsettled.

Words/phrase/sentence	Is there something jumping out and catching my attention? Am I getting a strong message? Am I imagining that I am there? Am I feeling anything?
The horizon was a puzzle	**A** – I'm interested because it is unusual. **M** – I'm getting the idea that the writer is confused. **I** – I am beginning to see lots of things that don't go together.
the jarring silhouettes	
grey concrete blocks	
flanked	

Explaining an effect

You must be able to:

* Understand how writers create effects
* Write an answer which clearly explains the way an effect has been created.

How are effects created?

Look closely at the following sentence:

> The grey scabbed turrets loomed precariously overhead as the children climbed the steep pathways cut like scars into the hillside.

The effect of this sentence is that it creates a feeling – a sense of foreboding; a distinct atmosphere.

But how does it do this?

Writers create effects with:

* The literal meaning of the words used (L).
* The implicit meanings created by the words used (I).
* The sensory images the words create (S).
* The **metaphor** which helps us to see the scene more clearly.

Now look at the sentence annotated to show each method in use: (L) for literal meaning, (I) for implicit meaning (S) for sensory images and (D) for language devices. Remember that some words can create more than one effect at the same time.

The grey (S) scabbed (I/S) turrets loomed precariously (L) overhead as the children climbed the steep pathways cut like scars (I/S/D) into the hillside.

SKILLS BUILDER 9

Now annotate the rest of the extract yourself, finding examples of four techniques that maintain the atmosphere.

> Arrow slits like the eyes of waiting dragons peered down on them and the portcullis lurked menacingly at the mouth of the keep, its teeth waiting hungrily for them to venture inside.

Writing about writer's effect

A good answer will always explain *how* the methods used by the writer create the effect stated.

Look closely at the sentences below and then complete the table.

> As they drew reluctantly closer, Aisha began to feel the heat of the molten lava convulsing in the castle moat singeing her eyebrows. Each coal glowed blood-red like poisonous rubies waiting to claim their prey.

Words/phrase selected	Method used	How it creates the effect
molten (lava)	Literal meaning Sensory images	Molten means to be made liquid by heat and suggests that it must be extremely hot and therefore dangerous, which continues the sense of foreboding.
(lava) convulsing	Literal meaning Sensory images Implicit meanings of words	
glowed blood-red	Implicit meanings of the words	
like poisonous rubies		
waiting to claim their prey	The implicit meanings of the words (personification)	The personification of the lava as 'waiting' for its prey, suggests that it has malicious intentions and wants to harm the children, which continues the sense of foreboding.

This can easily be written into a paragraph:

The phrase 'like lava convulsing' uses the literal meaning of the word 'convulsing' to help us to see the way the lava is moving in a jerky, rhythmic way. This detail also helps us to imagine it moving towards the children. The personification of the lava also makes us think that it wants to harm them. Finally, the words carry connotations of pain and illness, which are negative and add a sense of foreboding once again.

> Now write **two** paragraphs using your notes in the third and fourth rows of the table.

Revision tip

Remember that naming techniques such as **similes**, **metaphors** or other types of **figurative language** are useful but when explaining them you still need to refer to the **implicit** meanings or imagery that they create.

Exam-style practice questions

Read the passage below, which is taken from a short story by H.G. Wells called *The Red Room*. The story describes a man making his way to a room, which has become famous for its mysterious atmosphere and sense of danger.

And the passage I was in, long and shadowy, with a film of moisture glistening on the wall, was as gaunt and cold as a thing that is dead and rigid. But with an effort I sent such thoughts to the right-about. The long, drafty subterranean passage was chilly and dusty, and my candle flared and made the shadows cower and quiver. The echoes rang up and down the spiral staircase, and a shadow came sweeping up after me, and another fled before me into the darkness overhead. I came to the wide landing and stopped there for a moment listening to a rustling that I fancied I heard creeping behind me, and then, satisfied of the absolute silence, pushed open the unwilling baize-covered door and stood in the silent corridor.

The effect was scarcely what I expected, for the moonlight, coming in by the great window on the grand staircase, picked out everything in vivid black shadow or reticulated [marked in a net-like pattern] silvery illumination. Everything seemed in its proper position; the house might have been deserted on the yesterday instead of twelve months ago. There were candles in the sockets of the sconces, and whatever dust had gathered on the carpets or upon the polished flooring was distributed so evenly as to be invisible in my candlelight. A waiting stillness was over everything. I was about to advance, and stopped abruptly. A bronze group stood upon the landing hidden from me by a corner of the wall; but its shadow fell with marvelous distinctness upon the white paneling, and gave me the impression of someone crouching to waylay me. The thing jumped upon my attention suddenly. I stood rigid for half a moment, perhaps. Then, with my hand in the pocket that held the revolver, I advanced, only to discover a Ganymede and Eagle [a statue of characters from a Greek myth], glistening in the moonlight. That incident for a time restored my nerve, and a dim porcelain Chinaman on a buhl table, whose head rocked as I passed, scarcely startled me.

The door of the Red Room and the steps up to it were in a shadowy corner. I moved my candle from side to side in order to see clearly the nature of the recess in which I stood, before opening the door. Here it was, thought I, that my predecessor was found, and the memory of that story gave me a sudden twinge of apprehension. I glanced over my shoulder at the black Ganymede in the moonlight, and opened the door of the Red Room rather hastily, with my face half turned to the pallid silence of the corridor.

I entered, closed the door behind me at once, turned the key I found in the lock within, and stood with the candle held aloft surveying the scene of my vigil, the great Red Room of Lorraine Castle, in which the young Duke had died; or rather in which he had begun his dying, for he had opened the door and fallen headlong down the steps I had just ascended. There were other and older stories that clung to the room, back to the half-incredible beginning of it all, the tale of a timid wife and the tragic end that came to her husband's jest of frightening her. And looking round that huge shadowy room with its black window bays, its recesses and alcoves, its dusty brown-red hangings and dark gigantic furniture, one could well understand the legends that had sprouted in its black corners, its germinating darknesses. My candle was a little tongue of light in the vastness of the chamber; its rays failed to pierce to the opposite end of the room, and left an ocean of dull red mystery and suggestion, sentinel shadows and watching darknesses beyond its island of light. And the stillness of desolation brooded over it all.

Now answer this exam-style question.

1   **a)** Identify a word or phrase from the text which suggests the same idea as the underlined words below.

   (i) The man forced himself to think <u>logically</u>.

   (ii) He <u>imagined</u> that he could hear noises.

   (iii) Inside the room he almost started to move but then suddenly his eye was caught by what he thought was a figure crouching and he <u>halted quickly</u>.

   (iv) He felt a <u>pang</u> of fear as he opened the door to the Red Room.

   ....

   ....

   ....

   ....   **[4]**

continued on the next page

b) Using your own words explain what the writer means by the underlined words below:

And the passage I was in, long and shadowy, with a film of moisture glistening on the wall, was as <u>gaunt</u> and cold as a thing that is dead and rigid. But with an effort I sent such thoughts to the right-about. The long, drafty subterranean passage was chilly and dusty, and my candle flared and made the shadows <u>cower</u> and quiver. The echoes rang up and down the spiral staircase, and a shadow came sweeping up after me, and another <u>fled</u> before me into the darkness overhead.

....

....

....

....

....

.... **[3]**

c) Using your own words explain how the phrases underlined below are used by the writer to suggest the passage and its atmosphere that night.

And the passage I was in, long and shadowy, with a film of moisture glistening on the wall, was <u>as gaunt and cold as a thing that is dead and rigid</u>. But with an effort I sent such thoughts to the right-about. The long, drafty subterranean passage was chilly and dusty, and my candle flared and <u>made the shadows cower and quiver</u>. The echoes rang up and down the spiral staircase, and a shadow came sweeping up after me, and <u>another fled before me into the darkness overhead</u>.

....

....

....

....

....

.... **[3]**

d) Re-read the description of:

   (i) His journey to the room in paragraph 1.

   (ii) The room in paragraph 4.

Select four powerful words and phrases from each paragraph. Your choices should include imagery. Explain how each word or phrase selected is used effectively in the context.

Write about 200–300 words.

Up to 15 marks are available for the content of your answer.

[15]

Understanding extended response to reading questions

You must be able to:

- Understand how to approach extended writing type questions
- Look closely at the question to make sure your answer is focused in a useful way.

Knowing what to expect

Extended response questions test your ability to read a passage and select information in order to produce a piece of writing for a specific audience and purpose.

Extended writing tasks are usually laid out in a similar way.

Here is an example question with the key features labelled. (You do not need to look at **Passage A** yet as it is not needed in order to identify the key features of the question; they come from the wording of the task.)

Imagine that you are a 13-year-old student. (1) You and your parents have just attended the Open Evening of a new school opening in your area as described in **Passage A** and have decided you will go there. (2)

Write the transcript (3) of an interview between yourself, your parents and the Headteacher of your existing school (4) expressing your feelings about the possible school move. (5)

In your script you should:

- Explain what the new school is like.
- Explore your ideas and feelings about the new school and your parents' reaction to the idea of change.
- Discuss the possible effects of the decisions taken. (6)

Base your script on what you have read in **Passage A,** (7) but be careful to use your own words. (8) Address each of the bullet points. (9)

Begin your script: 'Good Morning Mrs Crane, I've got some exciting news. I've finally found the school for me!' (10)

You should write about 250–300 words, allowing for the size of your writing. (11)

Up to 15 marks will be available for the content of your answer (12) and up to 10 marks for the quality of your writing. (13)

Here is a summary of the key features identified in the question text.

1. The role you should write in.
2. The material you should use in your writing.
3. The form of writing you should create.
4. The audience for your writing.
5. The purpose of your writing.
6. The precise topics you should include in your writing.

7. A reminder that you must only use material from the passage in your answer.

8. A reminder that you should not copy out whole sentences.

9. A reminder that your answer must be balanced.

10. An opening sentence.

11. A word guide.

12. A reminder that the task is mainly testing your understanding of *what* you have read.

13. A reminder that there are some marks for *how* you write your answer.

SKILLS BUILDER 1

Go over some example questions in past papers and see if you can identify all 13 pieces of key information in them.

Using what you can work out from the question

Reading through the question carefully can help you to avoid pitfalls and succeed. Look at the diagram below, which shows how each of the 13 pieces of information can help you to improve your answer.

How it can help you
1. This will lead you to choose the correct **register** and voice.
2. This will keep your answer relevant.
3. This will help you to earn the 5 writing marks.
4. This will help you to create the correct level of formality.
5. This will help you to structure your writing.
6. This will keep your answer relevant.
7. This will keep your answer relevant.
8. This will keep your answer relevant.
9. This will help you to access all the content marks available.
10. This often contains hints about the attitude or angle you should develop in your answer.
11. This helps you to manage your time.
12. This will keep your answer relevant.
13. This will help you to gain the maximum marks available.

SKILLS BUILDER 2

Create a mnemonic to help you learn the 13 pieces of information to look out for when answering an extended response task.

Gathering information

You must be able to:

- Understand how to use the bullets in a question to create sub-headings for notes
- Understand how to make quick notes to capture important details.

Knowing what you need to find

Extended response questions usually tell you *what* to write about.

This information is featured in the bullets that are given within the task.

These bullets can be used as sub-headings for you to make notes under when you are reading the passage before you start your answer.

Look at the following example of a student's plan in response to a question. (You do not need to look at **Passage A** yet as you do not need to have it in order to practise analysing the way extended reading questions are usually laid out.)

Task

Imagine that you are the head teacher of the brand new school featured in the extract from a novel which is shown in **Passage A.**

Write the words of a speech for the school's first Open Day where the school will be promoted and places applied for.

In your script you should:

- Explain the school's philosophy and values.
- Outline the benefits of joining the new school.
- Explore your hopes for the future of the school.

Planning

What school believes in/wants

Positive effects of going there

How school will develop

SKILLS BUILDER 3

Now try making a set of sub-headings using the sample question below. (You do not need to look at **Passage B** yet as you do not need to have it in order to practise analysing the way extended reading questions are usually laid out.)

Imagine that you are one of a group of parents who attended the Open Day of a new school which opened in your town a few months ago. All of the parents took a tour guided by one of the school's first students, called Greta, an account of which is shown as **Passage B.**

Write the words of the letter that you write requesting a place for your child at the school.

In your letter you should:

- Give your impressions of the school.
- Explain your reasons for wanting a place for your child.
- Express your hopes for the future once your child is there.

Finding the information you will use in your writing

Once you have the sub-headings that you need to shape your notes, you are ready to start reading.

However, you can save yourself a lot of time and help yourself to be more successful if you make sure that your notes are brief but also include relevant details.

The best way to make sure that you keep to this rule is to make a grid for your notes before you start, like the one shown below.

Revision tip

Details are pieces of information such as:
- numbers
- names of places and people
- times and dates
- descriptions such as how something looked or sounded.

Sub-heading	Point	Detail
What school believes in/wants	Equality Opportunities for all	No bullying, e.g. use a bully court to resolve Same uniform for girls and boys – blue trousers Fund for students who cannot attend trips, e.g. trip to Paris
Positive effects of going to the school	Happy, confident	Doing assemblies
How the school will develop	Grow in popularity	More applications for next year

Create a set of notes for the sample question in the Skills builder on page 40. Use the extract below from **Passage B**, which would go with it.

A small, pale little girl stepped out in front of us and I almost groaned. "Oh no!" She wasn't going to be a convincing ambassador for this 'all singing all dancing wonder school' they were trying to sell us. "Welcome to my wonderful school. My name is Greta and I started here a term ago. I can't tell you how happy I am to be here today; especially as I was struggling in my last school and I never thought I'd be able to stand here in front of a group and speak like this. I've had so much help since I started here that I feel as if anything is possible now and I want your children to be able to say that one day too!" As she spoke she seemed to grow at least 10 centimetres taller and her voice seemed to resonate, far stronger than the rosebud mouth and freckled cheeks it flowered from.

"The thing is that everything here is about building up our confidence. From the very first day Mr Curtis explained that every lesson would include standing up and speaking in front of the class and that every assembly would include one student reading aloud or, if they were older, talking about a topic." She smiled around the room, drawing me in with her charm. "Do you know I did my talk on diabetes last week; because I've got it and I thought it'd be good to explain to everyone what it's like."

"It's not just the speaking though. I get a lot of help with my work, plus nobody laughs at you if you don't get it. You can put up a red card on your desk and the teaching assistant comes over and gives you a hand with it. You can put a green one up too – and then someone might ask you to help them if they're stuck. I felt really good yesterday helping someone with making plurals!" Greta continued to grow in stature before my eyes. Her shoulders were straighter, her stance firm.

Creating a role using voice and character

You must be able to:

- Write consistently in role
- Understand the importance of voice and character in creating a role
- Understand how to create character and voice in your writing.

What are role, character and voice?

Character is about a person's personality, values and beliefs.

A **role** is the part someone is playing, or the category they fit into; this could be their profession, their place in a group or a temporary state of mind. It will affect their purpose, what they think and what they talk about.

Voice is the particular personal expression and language that an individual uses. (This is often linked to their role but can also be linked to their character or even a temporary mood.)

SKILLS BUILDER 5

Copy out and sort the following words into three columns showing which could be used to describe roles, and their characters and voices.

(Parent)   (Teacher)   (Uses jargon)

(Uses slang and idioms)   (Uses a formal register)   (Uses Standard English)

(Friendly)   (Optimistic)   (Uses an informal register)

(Pessimistic)   (Student)   (Head teacher)

Why are role, character and voice important?

When completing an extended response question you will often write in role. It is important that you show that you have understood this and do not simply write as yourself.

To do this convincingly you need to alter your voice to match the person you are supposed to be.

Creating a character is hard to do in a short piece of writing but can make the fact that you are in role even more convincing.

How to get in role

The first step is to understand the role you have been placed in. Think about what a person in this role would spend their time doing and what is important to this type of person.

Next consider how they might feel about the topic you are writing about. Their role will have a big effect on their viewpoint and attitude.

Finally, decide whether they have a particular type of character and, if so, how that might be shown in a short piece of writing.

You can record these thoughts as quick notes or on a stick figure like the one on the right.

thoughts / attitudes

feelings

SKILLS BUILDER 6

Using the task outlined in the Skills builder on page 41, collect your thoughts about the role of the parent writing the letter.

How to create a voice

The final step when writing in role is to choose the language you will use. You have a series of choices:

- Formal or informal?
- **Jargon** or everyday language?
- Slang and idiom or **Standard English**?

SKILLS BUILDER 7

Draw lines to match the following sentences, which are all about impressions of a new school, to the roles given.

1. Prospective student persuading own parents	**a)** Having looked around the school I have been extremely impressed by the buildings, equipment and teachers that I saw.
2. Head teacher speaking to prospective parents / students	**b)** Wow! I mean you should see it … it's awesome … you'd just love it!
3. Parent applying for place for child at new school	**c)** Welcome to my wonderful school.
4. Current student speaking to tour of prospective parents / students	**d)** I am extremely proud to stand here today as the principal of this well resourced, well staffed institution, and welcome you on your journey to academic and personal success.

Organising and developing ideas in an extended response question

You must be able to:

- Understand the need to organise your ideas so that they are fluent and follow relevant conventions
- Understand the need to develop your ideas with detail and inference

Organising your answer

You should use the bullets given in the task. Very often these are organised into a logical order already.

Look again at the following task:

Imagine that you are one of a group of parents who attended the Open Day of a new school which opened in your town a few months ago. All of the parents took a tour guided by one of the school's first students, an account of which is shown as **Passage B** (page 41).

Write the words of the letter that you write requesting a place for your child at the school.

In your letter you should:

- Give your impressions of the school.
- Explain your reasons for wanting a place there.
- Express your hopes for the future once your child is there.

Look at the beginning of one student's plan below.

They have created a mind map for each bullet and have started to place ideas from the text around it.

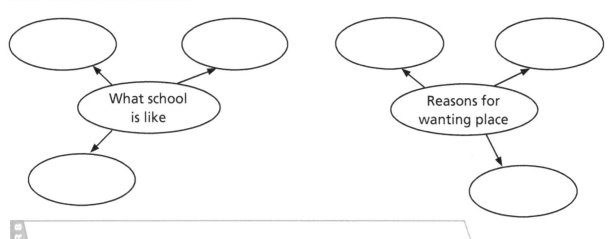

SKILLS BUILDER 8

Go back over a sample question and see if you can map out a plan using mind maps.

Using detail to develop an answer

It is important that you use details *from the text* to develop your answer. Do not be tempted to make things up as it is your reading that is being tested.

Look again at this extract from Greta's speech shown in Skills Builder 4.

Revision tip

You may be asked to write in one of the following forms: letter, report, journal, speech, interview, newspaper or magazine article; so it is important that you know the conventions of each of these.

> "The thing is that everything here is about building up our confidence. From the very first day Mr Curtis explained that every lesson would include standing up and speaking in front of the class and that every assembly would include one student reading aloud or, if they were older, talking about a topic." She smiled around the room, drawing me in with her charm. "Do you know I did my talk on diabetes last week; because I've got it and I thought it'd be good to explain to everyone what it's like."

One of the bullets to cover was:

- Give your impressions of the school.

You could write:

> It seems to build students' confidence
>
> You could develop this by adding:
>
> ... by getting them to do public speaking such as class presentations.
>
> You could even add:
>
> Our guide Greta had recently spoken about her diabetes in assembly and she seemed to have been really boosted by this.

Using inferences to develop an answer

It is also important that you add inferences that suit the role that you are writing in.

It may be that you personally would hate to be in a school where public speaking was an important element of the curriculum. However, most parents would consider this to be a useful life skill so would be very positive about this and consider it to be a very appealing feature of the school.

So you could add to the previous sentences even further:

> It seems to build students' confidence by getting them to do public speaking such as class presentations. Our guide Greta had recently spoken about her diabetes in assembly and she seemed to have been really boosted by this. I would really like my son to become more confident; he's quite shy at the moment and doesn't like speaking out in front of the class or anything. I worry about what sort of job he'll be able to do.

> **SKILLS BUILDER 9**
>
> Go over a past answer that you have given to an extended response task and identify **three** sentences that you can develop. Rewrite them adding additional details and inferences from the relevant text.

Exam-style practice questions

Read the extract below, then answer the exam-style questions.

Passage A

Creative School

My parents were never conventional and our schooling proved to be a fine example of their rejection of anything that would help me to blend in and disappear into a crowd.

My school was known locally as 'The Happy Hippy House' and was indeed started by some members of a band in the 1960s. The curtains (now a bit tattered and faded) had apparently started out as bright rainbow stripes and the building itself was once a fine private mansion, rather than a recognisably public institution. Term started with huge bunches of balloons being released from the top windows – a local event which we had never missed as youngsters.

If you happened to walk past 'T.H.H.H.' as it was fondly called, you would notice that it was never quiet. Electric guitars appeared to strum incessantly and the crashing of drums was an unavoidable menace. Yet many passers-by would pause and cock their heads, smiling with pleasure as a young voice soared sweetly, or the cacophony synchronised and a well-known hit filled the air. Tickets for the annual music and drama festival always sold out; and I'd spent many a summer's night curled up at my parents' feet getting an early taste of Shakespeare in between games of hide and seek in the wild gardens that surrounded the mansion house before I even set foot in a classroom there.

Actually, I did manage to gain a decent set of exam results. Despite the school's unusual facade, everyone took English and English Literature ("Why would you rob yourself of the tools of life boy? Why? Why? Why?" was the answer I got when I regularly begged to be released from English for extra band practice before a big concert). Maths was also compulsory – and there was plenty of daily practical learning on that score as we took bookings for performances, calculated our costs and set out invoices. T.H.H.H. was a business – and a profitable one at that. Talented students flocked there from neighbouring towns, to enjoy the extra hours of performing arts lessons which were available instead of other less glamorous subjects.

There were no barriers – boys could do ballet, girls played bass guitar. Most of us could dance, and everyone did their bit up on stage – you couldn't be shy for long when everyone was so encouraging. It's a confidence that has stayed with me to this day – and I wish I could bottle it and pass it on to my own children who seem so worried about what everyone thinks of them.

My favourite memories were of the 'show and tell' days when everyone was encouraged to bring a new piece, or for that matter, skill, to demonstrate in front of the class. There was often an air of secrecy about your offering and the school buzzed with excitement for days beforehand. It was at one of those sessions that I heard Shia Reece sing for the first time. (She went on to be signed by a record label and now lives somewhere in L.A. I'm told!) We all supported each other. I played the piano for Shia once (and have dined out on that story ever since!). She probably doesn't ever mention that she had a tiny bit-part in my first play, 'Solemn Starts', which launched my career when it was broadcast on the local radio and grabbed the attention of a producer driving his kids home from their swimming lessons!

I suppose it is true that the school took risks – we made our own sets and scenery for shows. And there was no such thing as healthy eating, but most of us missed meals frequently for rehearsals and gigs so it all evened out in the end. We travelled to concerts in a beaten-up school bus, until we bought a new one with the proceeds of a Summer Spectacular concert which featured a laser light show to music that some Year 11s had developed. But I don't remember anyone ever getting hurt – well, occasional cuts and bruises aside. We were always well supervised, sometimes by visiting stars who had come to visit the Principal of the school and inevitably got roped into whatever was going on at the time. Most memorably, hijacking my Geography lesson to describe a concert-tour of Alabama and the effects of flooding on local infrastructure!

1 Imagine that you are a student at a school in the same area as the 'Creative School' who has just read the extract in **Passage A**. Write your journal entry for that day explaining:

- What you think school life would be like there.
- How the school would help you to develop your artistic abilities.
- Do you think you will ever be a student there?

....

....

....

....

....

....

....

....

....

....

....

....

....

....

....

....

.... **[25]**

Understanding directed writing questions

You must be able to:

- Understand what directed writing questions are
- Understand the features of a successful response to a directed writing question.

Knowing what to expect

Directed writing questions ask you to read a text and evaluate the ideas that it contains before using them to create a new piece of writing.

Here is an example question with the key features labelled. (You do not need to look at **Passages A** and **B** as they are not needed in order to identify the key features of the question; they come from the wording of the task.)

Imagine that you are the aunt or uncle of twins; one girl and one boy. (1) You have just read the article about gender described in **Passage A** and the statistics found in **Passage B**. (2) Write a letter (3) to the writer (4) expressing your opinions of their views. (5)

In your letter you should:

- Summarise their views
- Evaluate their opinions
- Explore your ideas and feelings about what they have written. (6)

Base your letter on what you have read in **Passage A**, (7) but be careful to use your own words. (8) Address each of the bullet points. (9)

Begin your letter:
Dear Professor,
I read your article in *Science Monthly*, with interest. (10)

You should write 250–300 words, allowing for the size of your writing. (11)

Up to 10 marks will be available for the content of your answer (12) and up to 15 marks for the quality of your writing. (13)

Here is a list of the key features numbered 1–13.

1. The role you should write in.

2. The material you should use in your writing.

3. The form of writing you should create.

4. The audience for your writing.

5. The purpose of your writing.

6. The precise topics you should include in your writing.

7. A reminder that you must only use material from the passage in your answer.

8. A reminder that you should not copy out whole sentences.

9. A reminder that your answer must be balanced, which means that the whole passage must be used.

10. An opening sentence.

11. A word guide.

12. A reminder that the task is mainly testing your understanding of *what* you have read.

13. A reminder that there are some marks for *how* you write your answer.

Revision tip

Sometimes Directed Writing tasks can be based on one text of 650–750 words and on other occasions on two shorter texts totalling approximately 650–750 words. This may take you slightly longer to read, so prepare for this in your time planning.

Using what you can work out from the question

Reading through the question carefully can help you to be successful. Look at the table below, which shows how each of the 13 pieces of information can help you to improve your answer.

Piece of information	How it can help you
1. The role you should write in	This will lead you to choose the correct register and voice
2. The material you should use in your writing	This will keep your answer relevant
3. The form of writing you should create	This will help you to earn the 15 marks available for writing
4. The audience for your writing	This will help you to create the correct level of formality
5. The purpose of your writing	This will help you to structure your writing
6. The precise topics you should include in your writing	This will keep your answer relevant
7. A reminder that you must only use material from the passage in your answer	This will keep your answer relevant
8. A reminder that you should not copy out whole sentences	This will keep your answer relevant and save you time
9. A reminder that your answer must be balanced	This will help you to access all the content marks available
10. An opening sentence	This often contains hints about the attitude or angle you should develop in your answer
11. A word guide	This helps you to manage your time
12. A reminder that the task is mainly testing your understanding of *what* you have read	This will keep your answer relevant
13. A reminder that there are more marks for *how* you write your answer than showing what you have read	This will help you to gain the maximum marks available

Create a mnemonic to help you learn the 13 pieces of information to look out for.

SKILLS BUILDER 1

Gathering and synthesising information

You must be able to:

- Analyse the question to clarify exactly what information you need to find from the passage
- Use this understanding to create sub-headings for note-making
- Select and record points from more than one text.

Knowing what you need to find

Directed writing questions tell you *what* to write about.

This information is featured in the bullets that are given within the question.

These bullets can be used as sub-headings for you to make notes under when you are reading the passage before you start your answer.

Look at the following example of a student's planning in response to a task. (You do not need to look at **Passage A** yet as you do not need to have it in order to practise analysing the way directed writing questions are usually laid out.)

Question

Imagine that you are a nursery school owner and have read the guidelines on gender shown in **Passage A**. You decide to write an article for your nursery newsletter explaining the findings to parents and persuading them that they should adopt the recommendations.

Write your article, in which you:

- Explain what has been suggested.
- Why you do not agree.
- Discuss what parents should do next.

Planning

→ What the article suggests

→ Disagree

→ What next?

SKILLS BUILDER 2

Make a set of sub-headings using the question below.

Imagine that you are the parents of four children aged between 3 and 12. You have been listening to a radio programme about how to bring up your children without gender bias and have decided to try it. You decide to write to your own parents to inform them of your new parenting style and see if you can get them to alter their approach to their grandchildren.

Write the letter that you would send, in which you:

- Explain the beliefs and strategies you have decided to try.
- Give your opinion on the advantages of a bias-free approach.
- Anticipate their objections and fears about a bias-free approach and persuade them to your way of thinking.

Finding the information you will use in your writing

Once you have the sub-headings you need to shape your notes, you are ready to start reading.

However, you can save yourself a lot of time and help yourself to succeed if you make sure that your notes are brief but also include relevant details.

The best way to make sure that you keep to this rule is to make a grid for your notes before you start.

Look at the grid below, which was made in response to the following sample question:

Revision tip

Details are pieces of information such as:
- Numbers /times and dates
- Specific actions/items
- Names of places and people
- Descriptions, such as how something looks or sounds.

Imagine that you are a parent who has read a book about parenting. A section on career choice is printed below as **Passage A**. You decide to email the author to express your opinions about the points that they have made.

In your email you should:

- Specify what you agree with and why.
- Specify what you disagree with and why.
- Explain what you are going to do now you have thought about this issue.

Revision tip

This directed writing task could also feature two shorter passages, covering 650–700 words in total. If this is the case then you should still create a table but remember to fill it in using both texts, one after the other.

Sub-heading	Point	Detail
Things you agree with	Girls and boys should get the same careers advice.	Computer programs guiding careers choices should not ask the gender of the student using them.
Things you disagree with	Girls and boys should be dressed alike.	'Dungarees in a neutral colour should be compulsory.'
Your decisions / actions	To visit the children's school and check on careers advice given.	Look at toys in play room – do they show both genders if work-related? Ask about dressing-up box uniforms – are they gender-neutral, e.g. firefighter, not fireman?

Write a set of notes using the question set in Skills builder 2 on the text below. You have already created the sub-headings in a grid, as shown above.

Do you believe that you are a good parent? Think again ... Is your child's bedroom a pink palace or a parking lot? Is their wardrobe a jumble of froth and ribbons or a collection of mud brown and earth toned jeans and a full range of superhero t-shirts?

Your children are already being pre-conditioned by you. Do you know that 80 per cent of science, research engineering and technology professionals are male? Hmm, why could that be? How much time does your daughter spend tinkering on the car, building go-karts or grubbing around in the woods?

Creating a role using voice and character

You must be able to:
- Write consistently in role
- Understand the importance of voice and character in creating a role
- Understand how to create character and voice in your writing.

What are role, character and voice?

Character is about a person's personality, values and beliefs.

A **role** is the part someone is playing, or the category they fit into; this could be their profession, their place in a group or a temporary state of mind. It will affect their purpose, what they think about and what they talk about.

Voice is the particular, personal expression and language that an individual uses. (This is often linked to their role but can also be linked to their character or even a temporary mood.)

SKILLS BUILDER 4

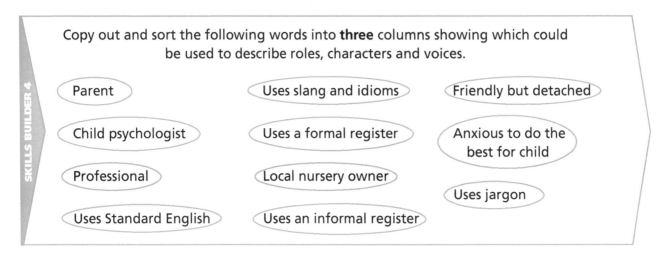

Copy out and sort the following words into **three** columns showing which could be used to describe roles, characters and voices.

- Parent
- Uses slang and idioms
- Friendly but detached
- Child psychologist
- Uses a formal register
- Anxious to do the best for child
- Professional
- Local nursery owner
- Uses jargon
- Uses Standard English
- Uses an informal register

Why are role, character and voice important?

When completing a directed writing question you will often write in role. It is important that you show that you have understood this and do not simply write as yourself.

To do this convincingly you will need to alter your voice to match the person you are supposed to be.

Creating a character is hard to do in a short piece of writing but can make the fact that you are in role even more convincing.

How to get in role

The first step is to understand the role you have been placed in. Think about what the person in this role would spend their time doing and what is important to this type of person.

Next consider how they might feel about the topic you are writing about. Their role will have a big effect on their viewpoint and attitude.

Finally, decide whether they have a particular type of character and, if so, how that might be shown in a short piece of writing.

You can record these thoughts as quick notes or on a stick figure like the one on the right.

thoughts / attitudes

feelings

SKILLS BUILDER 5

Make a stick figure to collect your thoughts about the role of the nursery owner in the question on page 50.

> **Revision tip**

Remember that although showing character is important, you must also evaluate the material contained in the passage, so do not allow yourself to become too one-sided or biased in your argument; always try to cover both positives and negatives, even if it is only to rebut those you disagree with.

How to create a voice

The final step when writing in role is to choose the language you will use. You have a series of choices:

- Formal or informal?
- Jargon or everyday language?
- Slang and idiom or Standard English?

SKILLS BUILDER 6

Draw lines to match the following sentences, which are all about the new guidelines regarding gender, to the correct roles.

1. New mum	a) This is ridiculous. Kids play with what they want to. When they come in here they make a beeline for the toys they want. I don't control that!
2. Nursery owner	b) Gender studies show that children absorb up to 45 per cent of their norms and values by the age of five.
3. Teenager studying psychology at college	c) I just want what's best for my child. I need to make sure they have the best chances and this stuff is stressing me out!
4. Toy shop owner	d) My duty is to share expertise with the parents whose children are in my charge and make sure that my employees are as up to date and on message as possible.

Answering a directed writing question

You must be able to:
- Understand the need to organise your ideas so that they are fluent and follow relevant conventions
- Understand the need to develop your ideas with detail
- Understand the importance of checking your spelling, punctuation and grammar.

How to organise your answer

The first thing to check is whether the type of writing you have been asked to write has any structural conventions. This task will ask you to write either a letter, speech or an article.

SKILLS BUILDER 7

> Make yourself a set of flashcards outlining the structural conventions of each type of writing.

Pay attention to the bullet points

You should always cover the material indicated by the bullets given in the task. However, simply following the order that they come in can create an unnatural structure and may not fit with the conventions you are following.

For instance, if you were approaching a task and were given the following three bullets:

1. Summarise their views.

2. Evaluate their opinions.

3. Explore your ideas and feelings about what they have written.

You could organise your writing so that it covers these in order: 1, 2, 3.

However, you may not want to sum up all of the points before evaluating a specific proposal or theory. Instead you could write a paragraph containing the first thing discussed in the article, then your analysis, then your thoughts and feelings about it, before returning to bullet 1 again and repeating the process. This would create a structure of 1, 2, 3, 1, 2, 3, 1, 2, 3, 1, 2, 3 and so on.

SKILLS BUILDER 8

> Go back over a sample question where you followed the bullets in sequence and see if you can re-structure your answer in a more sophisticated way.

How to use detail to develop an answer

It is important that you use details *from the text* to develop your answer. Do not be tempted to make things up as it is your reading that is being tested.

Remember that the focus of this directed writing task is evaluative. This means that the detail that you find is likely to consist of evidence and the way that you develop your answer further will be by analysing this evidence.

Look at this table of notes showing how a student developed two points taken from **Passage A**.

Point from text	Detail from text	Analysis
Toys are far less gendered than they used to be	Just two per cent of toys in a famous shopping catalogue were aimed at a single sex	Whilst this is positive, children do not buy from catalogues
Given the choice, children do not choose gendered toys	A recent study of one-year-olds showed that boys spent 46 per cent of their time playing with 'boy toys' and 37 per cent with 'girl' toys	This suggests that the problem doesn't exist if children have access to a mix of toys. So the real issue is with parents and what they purchase?

SKILLS BUILDER 9

Go over a past answer that you have given to a directed writing question and identify **three** sentences that you can develop. Re-write them using additional details from the relevant text.

Checking the accuracy of writing

This question is usually the only directed writing task to include marks for technical accuracy. This means that it is extremely important to build in time to proofread your work. Allow approximately five minutes for this.

Remember to check:

- Spelling. Double check, especially if you have used any unfamiliar vocabulary from the passage. Remove any text-speak, slang or inappropriate idioms.
- Punctuation. Make sure that every sentence begins with a capital letter and ends with a full-stop. Do not use commas instead of full-stops and avoid over-using exclamation marks.
- Grammar. Check that your subjects and verbs agree. Also check that you have written in the correct tense and that verbs are altered to match the tense.

Exam-style practice questions

Read **Passage A, Boys will be boys (or girls)**, an article about gender differences in toys and books for children, then answer Question **1**.

Passage A

Boys will be boys (or girls)

Is this all political correctness gone mad?

Campaigners say it's far more important than that. Despite the advances made in women's equality, the British economy – at least in some fields – remains starkly gender-baised. More than 80% of "science, research, engineering and technology professionals" are male; 82% of workers in "caring, leisure and other services" and 77% in administrative and secretarial roles are female. Developmental psychologists say that early ideas about gender – about being the "wrong sex" for certain careers or aspirations – can put children off for life. In any case it's not as if the relentless segregation of toys and books into girls' sections and boys' sections has always been so apparent.

Hasn't childhood always been defined along gender lines?

Never as overtly as today, when children's clothing stores are split between banks of blue and pink and the "girls" version of Scrabble comes with letters on the front spelling "FASHION". At the turn of the last century, barely any toys were aimed directly at girls or boys, says sociologist Elizabeth Sweet. In 1918, the American Ladies' Home Journal announced, after much debate, that "the generally accepted rule is pink for the boy, and blue for the girl", pink being "decided and stronger", blue "more delicate and dainty." True, things had changed by 1945, when around half of the toys in Sears, the US department store, were marketed for a specific gender, with girls encouraged to play little homemakers, and boys soldiers. But the 1960s and 1970s counterculture reversed that: by 1975, 68% of ads in the Sears catalogue were gender-neutral, with boys shown with toy kitchens and girls as aircraft pilots. Just 2% of toys were aimed at a single sex.

Why is it happening now?

The roles of men and women in society and at work are clearly less rigidly defined than they were 100 years ago, and one theory is that it's precisely because gender roles are breaking down that we seek to reinforce them in our children. The more cynical answer is that gender stereotypes are a bonanza for the British toy industry, which is worth £3bn a year. "The toy industry began to rely more heavily on market segmentation in the 1980s," says Sweet. "Why sell a family one version of a toy when you could sell two or more?" In 2012, Lego was accused of sexism for launching a pink "Lego Friends" range based on female figures, baking, parties and animals. But the company has refused to apologise. Lego Friends has driven its profits up by 35%. "Sales have been quite astonishing," says CEO Jørgen Vig Knudstorp.

So it's all about marketing, is it?

A lot of parents disagree, noting that an awful lot of it is based on common sense as well. "From as soon as she was able to walk my daughter seemed to like nothing better than pushing a baby dolly round in a pushchair," writes James Delingpole in the *Daily Express*. "My son at the same age was only interested in sitting around on his fat bottom, building things with bricks and smashing them up." The innate differences between boys and girls appear so obvious, it is pointless to deny them, argues Delingpole. "Is it really 'fantastic' to deny boys and girls the kind of toys they most want, just to demonstrate how enlightened and post-sexist you are?"

What do scientists say?

It's the old nature vs. nurture debate. There is evidence to suggest that girls and boys have innately different minds and preferences, and evidence that they do not. Primatologists point out that male and female monkeys (unaffected by the insidious influence of the media and advertising) also prefer different toys: males like things with wheels, females have broader preferences. Neuroscientists such as Lise Eliot, on the other hand, argue that infant brains are so malleable that gender is entirely constructed – often without us noticing. However it comes about, though, most studies show that baby boys and baby girls are not very different in how they interact with the world. A recent study of one-year-olds showed that boys spent 46% of their time playing with "boy" toys and 37% with "girl" toys – hardly an overwhelming preference.

So what does gender neutrality look like?

You only have to look at Sweden, where equal opportunities has been official policy in schools since 1998. There, nurseries try to balance and use gender-neutral toys, such as dinosaurs and animals. A new, neither male, nor female pronoun, "hen", is even being encouraged in early schooling and new children's stories. Campaigners say the proof is in the pudding: 13 out of Sweden's 24 government ministers are women (compared with four out of 22 Cabinet ministers in the UK). Women have almost equal working rights, Swedish men are more involved in childcare. According to Christine Ingebritsen, at the University of Washington, Sweden is already living in a "post-gender" future.

The Week, 5 April, 2014

continued on the next page

1. Read the article shown in **Passage A.**

Write a letter to an older friend or relative who is expecting their first child. You should cover:

- Your evaluation of the issues and solutions given.
- Your advice to them, which should attempt to persuade them to your way of thinking.

Base your letter on what you have read in Passage A, but do not copy from it.

Be careful to use your own words. Address each of the two bullet points.

Start your letter:

Hi there,

I bet you're so excited about the arrival of the baby soon. I know I'm hardly qualified to offer advice, but actually I just read a really interesting article …

You should write about 200–300 words.

Up to 15 marks are available for the content of your answer and up to 25 marks for the quality of your writing.

....

....

....

....

....

....

....

....

....

....

....

....

....

....

....

....

....

....

....

....

....

....

....

.... [40]

What is descriptive writing?

You must be able to:

- Understand the aims and purpose of descriptive writing
- Understand what the conventions of descriptive writing are.

What are the aims and purpose of descriptive writing?

Descriptive writing is writing which enables you to imagine that you are in the location or moment being written about. It should appeal to all of the reader's senses so that they can use this information to re-create the experience.

Descriptive writing does not have any purpose other than to help you to complete this re-creation. It is not about telling a story or conveying opinions and ideas.

Sometimes you will find descriptive writing as a part of a story, article or piece of persuasive writing, but in these cases it is being used to further the main purpose of those pieces, and this is probably not the kind of descriptive writing you will be asked to write.

SKILLS BUILDER 1

Read the three text extracts below. Which text extract could be a piece of exam-style descriptive writing? How do you know?

A: Picture the scene; the donkeys have been out to pasture all winter and their fur is matted and muddy – it has formed clumps and can no longer be combed out or smoothed. Their manes are tangled and twisted and even a kindly stroke gets caught up in knots and gnarls. Just a small donation could provide shelter for these poor creatures for the whole of the winter.

B: As I trudged towards my lessons that fateful day, I saw that Mr Jones' donkeys were still out in the fields. Their fur was matted and muddy – it had formed clumps and I could no longer comb it out or smooth it with my hands when they came to the hedgerow for the carrots Mum had given me. Their manes were tangled and twisted and even my kindly stroke got caught up in knots and gnarls. They had been there yesterday, and the day before that. In fact, I realised, they had been there for weeks. I resolved to visit the farm as soon as I got out of school.

C: The donkeys walk slowly towards me. Their fur is matted and muddy – it has formed clumps and can no longer be combed out or smoothed. Their manes are tangled and twisted and even a kindly stroke gets caught up in knots and gnarls.

Conventions of descriptive writing: imagery

Descriptive writing always helps you to visualise by creating imagery.

This can sometimes be achieved by using well selected words but is often created by using **figurative language**, e.g.:

The Sun shone fiercely like a raging fire in the sky – this comparison helps us to 'see' the colours of the Sun.

She jumped as high as a cheetah – this comparison helps us to 'see' the height of her jumps.

SKILLS BUILDER 2

Analyse how the following examples of figurative language help you to 'see'.

- We were hurtling towards the wall like a comet through the sky.
- The baby beamed; its cheeks were like rosy apples.

Conventions of descriptive writing: adjectives and adverbs

Descriptive writing also contains **adjectives** and **adverbs**, which stimulate your brain so that it can re-create what each of your other senses: hearing, touch, taste, and smell would experience if you were there. It may also provoke your emotions. For example:

The house smelt dank and musty as I pushed open the door. Spread across the scratched oak table, the remains of an evening meal, now days old, seemed covered in a white fur blanket. Peaks of muddy gravy-clad potato pierced it here and there, and the vivid green of once freshly picked peas was dulled under a blue-grey haze. Aware of a scrabbling noise, I stumbled awkwardly backwards and watched as tiny mice fled from the nest of shredded paper napkins they had constructed in the shadow of the tarnished old teapot.

SKILLS BUILDER 3

Using different colours, annotate the passage above to show which words provoke each one of your five senses.

Conventions of descriptive writing: information, not story

Descriptive writing is **structured** so that that each paragraph gives more information about a person, place or moment, rather than building up a story by introducing a new event or developing our understanding of a character or relationship.

Developing descriptive writing

You must be able to:

- Understand how to sequence a piece of descriptive writing
- Understand how to develop descriptive writing.

How is descriptive writing structured?

Descriptive writing is structured so that the reader's focus is on *what they can imagine*, rather than on what is *happening*.

To do this, writers choose to organise their writing in a way which does not place a sequence of events in the foreground.

Instead they can:

- *Focus on a very narrow moment in time*; a little like a single snapshot from a camera, e.g.:

> As the hurricane hit I saw metal spew from the building in flashing spirals, corkscrew curls of aluminium sheeting as they ripped from the roof and hurtled outwards towards the blackening sky. Seconds later icy shards of window fell to the ground as the windows bowed and broke.

- *'Stay' in one place and describe what is around them,* almost as if they are moving a camera to make a film, e.g.:

> As I look around me I can see the russet leaves on the trees falling to the ground. Scanning the forest floor, I see more and more colours; heaps of gold and auburn as they frolic in the breeze and form banks along the edges of the path.

- *Describe the same object / person / place but from different time perspectives,* e.g.:

> My grandmother today is like a sepia photograph; pale and washed out, the contours of her face blurred by wrinkles and folds so that I have to look hard to find the face I used to know. Then her nose was narrow, almost beak-like, and her eyes twinkled bright, bright, blue sapphire not the milky, flat agate of her later years. Then her hair was silky and flyaway, always being tugged in exasperation as she brushed it out of her eyes. Now it is dry and clings flat to her head, matt and greyed as if tired of adventure.

- *Select two seasons or other moments of high contrast* such as in sunshine and in a storm, or night and day, to describe the same place, e.g.:

By day the shopping centre is an ant nest of activity; buzzing as the cars come and go, the tills ring up over and over and the shoppers make circuits with eager smiles. By night it is a different story – empty caverns echoing with the trickle of fountains never heard in opening hours. Car parks full of shadows and dark corners, where litter congregates to mutter in the night winds.

SKILLS BUILDER 4

Rewrite one of the descriptions above using an alternative way of structuring the description.

How is descriptive writing developed?

The key to developing a piece of descriptive writing is to add detail.

Instead of stating something factually and briefly, think about using additional information about what can be seen and also using adjectives and adverbs to stimulate each of the reader's senses instead of just one sense.

Look at the table to see how you could develop the simple phrase below into a paragraph.

A horse is in the field.

	Add an adjective/adverb	Add an example of figurative language occasionally
Add how it looks	A *brown* horse	Its coat was as glossy as a conker.
Add what it was doing	It grazed nervously. Head flicking from side to side anxiously.	not applicable
Add how it moves	Stepping gingerly through the grass …	As if the earth was hot beneath his hooves.
Add how it 'feels' to the touch	His coat was thick and smooth …	Like a fine blanket.
Add the sounds that it makes	His breath was loud and wet sounding as it left his nostrils …	not applicable
Add the smells that come with it	The scent of saddle soap and leather wafted gently from his coat …	not applicable
(Add any tastes if relevant)	not applicable	not applicable

SKILLS BUILDER 5

Use the table above to develop the phrase below. Remember that figurative language and taste may be relevant and other senses may <u>not</u> be in your writing.

The old woman stood on the cliff.

Using imagery and sensory detail in a description

You must be able to:

- Select an effect to guide your word choices
- Choose words that stimulate the senses
- Understand how to sustain an effect with imagery and sensory detail.

Deciding what effect you are aiming for

Writers aim to create one or more of the effects below in their writing.

1. To gain and keep attention.
2. To provoke a reaction.
3. To convey an idea, attitude, emotion or mood / atmosphere.
4. To create a sensory picture.

In descriptive writing the focus is on effects 3 and 4. The first decision you need to make is what emotion or mood / atmosphere you wish to create.

Sometimes there will be a clue in the title or task that you are given, e.g.:

- Describe a room filled with sadness. Sombre atmosphere and sad emotions.

- The day of the results! Tense mood and mixed emotions.

Other titles are more open and leave the decisions completely up to you, e.g.:

- Returning home Tense mood and nervous emotions/excited mood and happy emotions.

- The hilltop cottage Sense of foreboding and fear/atmosphere of contentment and relaxation.

SKILLS BUILDER 6

Decide which effects you would aim for if writing a response to the tasks or titles below:

- Write a description of a celebration
- Waiting at the dentist
- The party
- The castle
- A typical villain

Choosing words which stimulate the senses

Word choice is vital to creating a description. You need to select words so that their meanings are very precise and give as much information as possible about whatever you are describing.

For instance, instead of writing 'house' you should use more precise words as some words carry additional details that your reader will instantly use to help them to imagine the scene.

Look at the table below, which shows the information conveyed by some alternatives to the word 'house'.

Word	Literal meaning	Associations	Possible atmospheres
mansion	Large and grand building	Wealth, upper class, celebrity	Intimidating. Could be scary if very large and uninhabited
shack	Small, tumbledown dwelling	Poor, wood, broken windows	Sense of neglect / sombre atmosphere
lair	Secret place. Home for an animal	Crime? Place for someone to hide	Fear and tension

How to sustain an effect: imagery and sensory detail

When you are choosing imagery and sensory detail you need to make sure that it creates the correct effect and also matches the effect of other words used. Choosing the correct word or image depends upon the associations of the words.

Imagine that you are writing about a dancer in a show. Look at the possible similes that could be used and their associations.

The girl moved across the stage like:

Word	Association
a) A butterfly	Delicate, fast moving, seems to hover
b) A spider	Small, light, swift moving, scary
c) A gazelle	Slim, fast moving, nervous and moves abruptly

If you wanted to suggest that the girl was graceful and attractive you would choose **a)** but if you wanted to suggest that she seemed to lack confidence, you might choose **c)**.

SKILLS BUILDER 7

When might you choose to complete the simile with **b)**?

How to sustain an effect: semantic field

The best descriptive writing not only creates an overall effect but also links the language and images used by drawing them from the same **semantic field**.

For example, you could choose to describe someone using images and language linked to boats and the sea:

She swept through the classroom like a majestic yacht, cutting through the waves of students and coming to rest smoothly at her desk.

SKILLS BUILDER 8

Describe a busy office using images related to bees and a hive.

Exam-style practice questions

Here are two descriptive questions. Choose one question from **Set A** and answer it under timed conditions – allow yourself 60 minutes to answer the question. Write about 350–450 words.

Set A

1 Describe a moment from a music festival or sporting event that you have attended.

....
....
....
....
....
....
....
....
....
....

.... **[40]**

(You will need to continue on a separate piece of paper.)

or

2 'The Meeting'. Write a description, using this as your title.

....
....
....
....
....
....
....
....
....

.... **[40**

(You will need to continue on a separate piece of paper.

An additional set of questions are provided below so that you can continue to practise your skills using a range of titles.

Set B

1 Write a description of a person who scares you.

....

....

....

....

....

....

....

....

....

....

....

.... **[40]**

(You will need to continue on a separate piece of paper.)

or

2 'The old hospital'. Describe a walk around this abandoned building.

....

....

....

....

....

....

....

....

....

....

....

.... **[40]**

(You will need to continue on a separate piece of paper.)

What is narrative writing?

You must be able to:

- Understand the aims and purpose of narrative writing
- Understand the conventions of narrative writing.

What are the aims and purpose of narrative writing?

Narrative writing is writing which tells a story by creating a sequence of events and a group of characters who experience them, in a way which engages our empathy and interest. It includes dialogue and description that should appeal to all of the reader's senses so that they can use this information to re-create the experience and explore the themes that are suggested.

SKILLS BUILDER 1

> Read the two text extracts below. Which text could be an extract from the start of a piece of exam-style narrative writing? How do you know?
>
> **A:** Sera trudged through the city, her eyes glistening with tears, blurring the outlines of glossy parcels stacked in the gaily dressed show windows. The smell of pine needles filled her senses as she brushed past trees leaning nonchalantly against the walls of the subway station. It was too late. Too late to catch the train, race to the airport and stop him from leaving her forever.
>
> **B:** The Christmas windows sparkle with glitter and shiny metallic papers and the glass seems to bow and bulge as the commuters' eyes water in the cold air. Tall, black green needles of pine brush against their coats as the trees lean nonchalantly against the subway station entrance and the scent of pine fills everyone's nostrils.

What are the conventions of narrative writing?

Narrative writing tends to follow these conventions.

1. Contains a sequence of events.
2. These events often present a problematic situation and then work towards this coming to a climax and resolution.
3. Relies upon characters to 'show' how the story unfolds as well as a narrator to 'tell'.
4. Characters are well described so that readers are able to empathise with them and become more engaged with the narrative as a whole.
5. Contains descriptive detail in order to make settings and characters vivid so that the reader can become involved.
6. Utilises dialogue to develop the reader's understanding of events, characters and relationships.

Organise the notes below into two separate plans for two stories titled:

- The Disaster
- The Meeting

A girl receives a letter from a girl who says she is her twin.	Setting: Rainy day in a small city apartment in Paris.	Narrator: First person, female	Setting: Hot summer in large rambling country house in Wales.
Grandson smells smoke when talking to grandmother and rushes out to alert workman.	Grandson calls to see elderly grandmother and offers to make her a drink.	Characters: Girl, 18, and her mother, who is a single parent.	She searches her mum's drawers and finds a birth certificate.
Girl is shocked and upset but realises her mother had to make a difficult choice and accepts this.	She asks her mother about it but her mother gets angry and walks out.	Grandson finds workman, who has injured his leg. Calls ambulance.	Characters: Elderly resident, grandson, 17. Workmen re-roofing older part of apartment.
Grandson stumbles and gets foot caught in roofing. Struggles but gets free.	Workman is working on roofing but falls off ladder to ground and is hurt but nobody can see / hear him.	Her mum comes back and sees the birth certificate so they talk about what happened.	Grandson climbs onto roof to put out fire.
They go together to meet the twin.	Grandson returns to grandmother who wants more tea.	Blowtorch being used on roof sets the timbers alight.	Narrator: First person, male

How is narrative writing structured?

You must be able to:

- Understand how to sequence a piece of narrative writing
- Understand how to develop narrative writing.

How narrative writing is sequenced: structure

Narrative writing is structured so that the reader's focus is on what is *happening* rather than what they can *imagine*.

To do this, writers choose to organise their writing in a way which places events in the foreground; it is the events that lead us forward and link each section of the writing to the next.

1. Introduction	2. Rising action	3. Climax	4. Falling action	5. Resolution
Setting and characters are introduced	Events occur, which lead to a climax of some kind	An event which brings everything to a head/crisis occurs	Solutions to the events that have happened are found	Everything is rounded off and all loose ends tied up

SKILLS BUILDER 3

Think of a famous story or narrative that you know well and see if you can split it into the five parts listed above.

How narrative writing is sequenced: openings

Narratives start with a strong opening to hook the reader. This usually establishes the setting, characters and a key event that may set off a chain of other events or hint at events to come.

How narrative writing is sequenced: endings

Narratives close with an ending that draws the events of the story to a close or resolution, or deliberately creates a cliffhanger for a continuation of the story.

Some ways that narratives can be made even more successful is to 'play' with the structure. For instance, the story could start with the crisis and then flash back to how it came about. It could even start with the resolution and then begin again at the beginning, unfolding the events which led to it. A 'twist', which means that things do not turn out as expected, is also a good way to inject originality into your story.

How is narrative writing developed?

The key to developing a piece of narrative writing is to add detail and dialogue so that what is happening is shown, rather than told.

Instead of stating something factually and briefly, think about adding additional information about the setting and characters, as well as dialogue to bring the situation to life and add further detail.

Look at how you could develop the simple sentence below into a paragraph.

Pieter walked into the office and waved the sheaf of bills in front of Igor's face.

Add detail	What it adds
Pieter stalked into the ramshackle office, slamming the scratched and peeling door hard against the door frame.	This tells us what things looked like but also suggests that the business may not be profitable or that it is badly managed.

Add dialogue	What it adds
'How long did you think you could keep these hidden away then?' Pieter spoke rapidly and with an edge of steel but his voice shook as he scowled down at Igor.	This tells us that Igor has been dishonest and suggests that Pieter is furious but also distressed, suggesting that it is his business too, or that it matters to him greatly.

Add detail and dialogue for the next part of the sentence:

Igor looked up slowly from the pile of letters and ledgers covering his desk and brushed his hair out of his tired eyes.

SKILLS BUILDER 4

Creating character and setting

You must be able to:

- Choose effective words to describe characters and settings
- Use dialogue to create a sense of character and relationship.

Choosing effective words to describe characters and settings

Although you must be careful not to confuse descriptive and narrative writing, it is important to include descriptive details in a narrative because they are what bring characters and places alive for your readers.

It is also far more effective to 'show' rather than 'tell' a story.

However, it is not wise to give these details all at once or to make them the sole point of a sentence or paragraph.

Note how the following text extract blends *details* in between *dialogue* and *events*. This extract is from a psychological thriller called *The Water's Lovely* and is a key moment in the story, where Edmund's mother tries to 'match-make'.

'Absolutely delicious, Irene,' said Marion, no mean cook herself in her own estimation. She had brought a Bakewell tart with her as a gift. 'If I shut my eyes I might be in Bologna.'

'I wish you were' thought Edmund. So it was Irene now. Last time she was here they had still been on 'Mrs Litton' terms. Marion's hair was redder and darker than it had been at the beginning of the week and her little marmoset face more brightly painted. He had never known a woman be such a fidget. She couldn't sit still for five minutes but was up and down, bouncing about on her little stick legs and her kitten heels.

'You mustn't think you have to come with me,' she said to him when she had served and cleared away the coffee. Another first time.

'It's no trouble,' said his mother as if she were doing it herself.

The Water's Lovely, Ruth Rendell, 2006

We learn a lot about his mother from the extract, and also about Edmund, from his reactions. We also find out about Marion: that she dyes her hair, that she is wearing more make-up than she used to and that she is a fidget.

SKILLS BUILDER 5

What do we infer about Marion from the details that we have been given?

This extract is taken from later in the novel, where Edmund has invited a colleague out to the cinema in order to show his mother that she cannot choose a girlfriend for him.

'This is Heather, Mother,' Edmund said.

'How do you do?'

The girl said 'Hello Mrs Litton' in the sort of tone too casual for Irene's liking.

Nice hair, thought Irene, but otherwise nothing much to look at. 'Can I get you some tea?'

'We're going to the cinema,' the girl said.

'How nice. What are you going to see?'

'The Manchurian Candidate.'

'Oh I'd love to see that,' said Irene.' Nicole Kidman's in it, isn't she?'

'I don't think so.' Heather turned from Edmund to face her with a smile. 'Will you excuse us, Mrs Litton? We have to go. Come on, Ed, or we'll be late.'

Ed! No one had ever called him that …

The Water's Lovely, Ruth Rendell, 2006

It is clear from the brief answers that Heather gives, that she is not interested in making friends with Mrs Litton. It is also clear by the way that she says 'Hello' rather than 'how do you do' and abbreviates Edmund's name that she is a more relaxed, less formal person than Mrs Litton would like.

SKILLS BUILDER 6

Look back at the dialogue in the first text extract. What does it show you about Marion and about Mrs Litton?

Exam-style practice questions

Composition questions – narrative

Here are **two** sets of composition questions. Choose one question from **Set A** and answer it under timed conditions – allow yourself 60 minutes to answer the question. Write about 350–450 words.

Set A

1. 'The Accident'. Write the dramatic part of a story which involves an accident of some kind.

....

....

....

....

....

....

....

....

.... **[40]**

(You will need to continue on a separate piece of paper.)

or

2. 'The Journey'. Write the opening chapter of a story with this title.

....

....

....

....

....

....

....

....

....

....

.... **[40]**

(You will need to continue on a separate piece of paper.)

An additional set of questions are provided below so that you can continue to practise your skills using a range of titles.

Set B

1 Write the ending to a story titled: 'The Fire'.

....

....

....

....

....

....

....

....

....

....

....

.... **[40]**

(You will need to continue on a separate piece of paper.)

or

2 Write the first half of a short story about a person or animal who needs to be rescued.

....

....

....

....

....

....

....

....

....

....

.... **[40]**

(You will need to continue on a separate piece of paper.)

Answers

The marking guidance and example answers included in this section are written by the author. In examinations, the way marks would be awarded may be different.

1. Comprehension questions	
Understanding comprehension questions	
Skills builder 1	
1.	E
2.	E
3.	E
4.	(i) I (ii) I
5.	E
6.	I
Skills builder 2	
1.	Explain in your own words
2.	Explain in your own words
3.	Give / identify
4.	(i) Explain in your own words (ii) Explain in your own words
5.	Give / identify
6.	Explain in your own words
Skills builder 3	
1.	Using your own words **explain** what the writer meant by: 'the result seems very robust'.
2.	**Explain** what scientists used to believe was the cause of the decline of dinosaurs on Earth.
3.	**Identify** the evidence which was used as the basis of the new theory.
4.	Using your own words **explain** what the text means by: (i) 'already past their prime' (ii) 'under stress'
5.	**Give** two reasons why scientists believe that dinosaurs died out on Earth.
6.	**Explain** what the writer meant by 'some kind of long death march'.
Answering short answer questions	
Skills builder 4	
3.	**Re-read paragraph 4 and** Identify the evidence which was used as the basis of the new theory.
4.	Using your own words explain what the text means by: (i) 'already past their prime' **(line 15)** (ii) 'under stress' **(line 19)**
5.	**Re-read paragraph 1.** Give two reasons why scientists believe that dinosaurs died out on Earth.
6.	Explain what the writer meant by 'some kind of long death march'. **(line 27)**

1. Comprehension questions	

Skills builder 5

1.	The results seem strong and very unlikely to be refuted.
2.	A meteorite impact/giant asteroid which hit the Earth.
3.	Benton's models of the rates of dinosaur speciation events.
4.	(i) not as healthy and strong a species as they had been (ii) suffering problems and having to battle to survive
5.	1) a galactic catastrophe 2) a slow and steady decline of the species
6.	That they had been declining towards extinction slowly, for ages.

Answering questions which require inference

Skills builder 6

	Quote	shift in their seats	begin to tap repeatedly	begins and then halts	looking quickly around the room
	Means	Moving around in their seats.	Move their pens and laser pointers and strike the table.	He starts to speak and then stops again.	He tries to see who is around him.
	Suggests	Uncomfortable psychologically as well as physically/ wish they could go.	They are agitated.	He is anxious about how his words will be received/does not wish to speak.	He is nervous about who might hear what he has to say.

Skills builder 7

He does not share the beliefs of the people who say that dinosaurs died out because of factors other than the asteroid, and wants to disagree but is worried because of the fact that not many people agree with him.

Exam-style practice questions: Comprehension questions

1.	Cuban solenodon
2.	(i) They think it will never be found again. (ii) To treat it badly for no reason. (iii) Areas which are a long way from civilisation.
3.	a) Not enough of the species left to keep it going b) Habitats too small to sustain life of species
4.	Hundreds of people have gone looking. A novel was written about it. A film was made about it.
5.	He was disappointed as he had wanted it to be true.
6.	It is a scientific thrill. There are sometimes rewards. It is an emotional / powerful quest.

2. Summary writing questions

Understanding summary questions

Skills builder 1

Use this checklist to see if the question you have written fulfils the criteria for a complete question.

Part 1

Have you given a focus?

Have you said where to look for material?

Have you reminded students that own words are not necessary?

Have you said how many marks are available?

Have you given bullets?

Part 2

Have you explained how to write up the answer?

Have you stated that it should be in continuous prose?

Have you said how much they should write?

Have you said how many marks are available?

Preparing for summary questions

Skills builder 2

Possible answer:

Sentence 1: The ice cave season in Iceland is rather short or from November to March.

Does this tell me a preparation that they made?	**No**
Can I infer that a preparation was made?	**No**
Do I learn anything about preparations at all?	**Yes** – they may need to plan when to go as there aren't many chances.

Sentence 2: Outside of that season it can be dangerous to go into the caves because they can collapse, which is, well, dangerous.

Does this tell me a preparation that they made?	**No**
Can I infer that a preparation was made?	**No**
Do I learn anything about preparations at all?	**Yes** – they must check it is the best season.

Sentence 3: I'm guessing the reason is that it's not cold enough.

Does this tell me a preparation that they made?	**No**
Can I infer that a preparation was made?	**No**
Do I learn anything about preparations at all?	**No**

Sentence 4: So if a visit to an ice cave is on the top of your Iceland bucket list, the window is small.

Does this tell me a preparation that they made?	**No**
Can I infer that a preparation was made?	**No**
Do I learn anything about preparations at all?	**Yes** – you should plan so you don't miss the window of opportunity.

2. Summary writing questions	
Skills builder 3	
Main idea: clothing layers, microfibre	
Examples/detail: vest, sweater, fleece, gloves, thermal underwear	
Writing in summary style	
Skills builder 4	
Possible groupings: things for you to do / things for others to do / safety concerns / skill issues.	
Skills builder 5	
I am going to write about advice to give tomb-stoners. (C) I think tomb-stoners are mad (O) but if they're going to do it then I think the least they can do is to check the alluring cliffs online first and see if they have a bad safety record; either injuries, cliff erosions or sea issues. (E) The thing is, if they don't wear a knife and goggles (D) then they can't cut themselves free of any rope or weeds they might land in (C), if there is any trouble (which is stupid (O)) and if they haven't booked lifeguards or friends to keep a lookout then they're really on their own if they've got injured by hitting rocks or the bottom. (C) This would be my advice. (C)	
Exam-style practice questions: Summary writing questions	

1	Mark scheme for summary writing question	
	13–15	Your answer is focused on the daredevils passage and on the challenges that they faced. You have used your own words when possible and have written in a clear, concise and fluent style (without examples or comment).
	10–12	Your answer is mostly focused on the daredevils passage but you may have added some comments or opinions or an introduction and conclusion, which are not necessary. You have used your own words and written clearly and concisely most of the time.
	7–9	Some of your answer is focused on what you have learned about the challenges for the climbers but sometimes you lose focus. You have listed ideas rather than organising them into clear groups. Sometimes your answer is not clear or concise.
	4–6	Your summary is sometimes focused on the challenges faced by the climbers but you add too much unnecessary information and it is long and may feature copying out.
	1–3	Your summary does not focus on the challenges faced by the men and is too wordy. You have not used a summary style and may have copied out a lot of information.
	0	Your answer is unfocused and features a lot of copying out. It may not be possible to understand your answer.

3. Short answer and language questions

Showing that you understand literal meanings

Skills builder 2

Sentence given: His mother always got the <u>same</u> type of presents.

Step 1: Synonyms: like / similar / share qualities

Step 2: look for gifts / presents

Step 3: predictable

Sentence given: He wanted the day to be <u>less routine and mundane</u>.

Step 1: Synonyms : traditional / habitual / normal

Step 2: look for day

Step 3: special

Skills builder 3

Word underlined: meticulousness

Step 2: careful / attention to detail / precise

Step 3: He planned the party very carefully and with attention to small details.

Word underlined: dictated

Step 2: prescribed / ordered / told

Step 3: He had given very strict instructions about the birds' design.

Showing that you understand implicit meanings

Skills builder 4

	Phrase	Implicit meaning/associations
	military meticulousness	Negative? Not much warmth or feeling? Consider it very important – life or death – perhaps a bit too much?
	rigidly dictated	Negative? A bit bossy? Not very warm or pleasant?

Understanding language questions

Understand what 'powerful words' means
A = 4,   B = 3,   C = 4,   D = 1

Skills builder 6

	To gain and keep attention	To provoke a reaction	To convey an idea, attitude, emotion or mood	To create a sensory picture
	Clawed is usually associated with an animal so catches our attention due to this mismatch.	The idea that a child is so unhappy is alarming and makes us instantly sympathetic.	Clawed and whined suggest sadness and desperation to escape / gain attention, which suggest that the boy feels this way.	Shredding and vicious splinters show us what the wood looked like and also suggest the boy's pain.

Identifying an effect and selecting the words which show it

Skills builder 8

Words / phrase / sentence	Is there something jumping out and catching my attention? Am I getting a strong message? Am I imagining that I am there? Am I feeling anything?
The horizon was a puzzle	A – I'm interested because it is unusual. M – I'm getting the idea that the writer is confused. I – I am beginning to see lots of things that don't go together.
the jarring silhouettes	A – I'm interested because it is unusual. M – I'm getting the idea that the writer may not like what he/she is seeing. I – I am still seeing lots of things that don't go together. I also wonder if the sky is bright and the buildings are dark. F – I'm beginning to feel very curious – what is it the writer doesn't like?
grey concrete blocks	I – I can 'see' specific colours and shapes. M – grey seems a bit dull and depressing. I'm getting the message that the writer isn't uplifted by what he / she sees.
flanked	I – I can 'see' the way the buildings have been built very closely together.

Explaining an effect

Skills builder 9

Arrow slits (S) like the eyes of waiting dragons (I/D) peered (L) down on them and the portcullis lurked (L) menacingly (L) at the mouth of the keep, its teeth (L) waiting hungrily (I) for them to venture inside.

Skills builder 10

How you complete the table will depend on what you think about the text. Here are some possible notes.

Words/phrase selected	Method used	How it creates the effect
(lava) convulsing	Literal meaning Sensory images Implicit meanings of words	Convulsing means to move in a sudden distinct spasm which suggests that the lava is progressing in fits and spurts. The word is associated with pain which suggests a negative atmosphere and a sense of foreboding; that the lava may be hurtful and destructive.
glowed blood-red	Implicit meanings of the words	Blood is implicitly linked with danger, which adds to the sense of threat from the lava.

like poisonous rubies	Literal meaning Sensory images Implicit meaning of words	'Poisonous' means that something can make you very ill and could possibly kill you. This suggests that the coals are life-threatening. Rubies are red-coloured stones, which helps to create a visual effect but also implies that the moat is full of rare and precious things; this adds to the sense of being in a fantastic, unusual place.

Here are possible answer paragraphs.

'Glowed blood-red' gives us a clear visual picture of the scene but also because of the implicit links with injury and death that the word 'blood' brings, suggests a sense of threat and danger and makes the reader worried for the girl.

'Poisonous rubies' continues to provide a clear visual picture of the redness of the lava and the separate clumps that it has formed into. However, it also suggests a sense of threat because the coals are said to be poisonous, which we know is often deadly. The simile of rubies creates an other-worldy feel as it is unlikely that there would be so many precious jewels in one place.

Exam-style practice questions: short answer questions and language task

(a)	i) sent such thoughts to the right-about (para 1) ii) I fancied (para 1) iii) stopped abruptly (para 2) iv) twinge (para 3)
(b)	gaunt – unhealthily thin cower – make oneself low and small in fear fled – to run away in fear
(c)	Award one mark up to a maximum of 3: • The passage feels unpleasant. • The passage is eerie. • The atmosphere seems threatening / intimidating. • There is a sense of foreboding.
(d) (i)	

Choice	Explanation
long and shadowy / the darkness ahead	Visual effect but also connotations of fear as vision not clear due to length of room and darkness.
film of moisture glistening	Visual effect

gaunt and cold as a thing that is dead and rigid	Simile: sensory appeal – temperature but also connotations of fear at mention of dead thing. Creates atmosphere of foreboding.
long, drafty subterranean passage	Visual effect but also connotations of fear as vision not clear due to length of room and darkness.
chilly and dusty	Visual / sensory effect with negative connotations as cold links with discomfort.
my candle flared and made the shadows cower and quiver	Visual effect but also connotations of fear as vision not clear due to length of room and darkness.
echoes rang up and down	Sensory appeal: hearing – creates tense atmosphere and feelings of fear as there should not be echoes.
a shadow came sweeping up after me / another fled before me	Visual effect creates tense atmosphere and feelings of fear as there should not be shadows.
a rustling … creeping behind me	Sensory appeal: hearing creates tense atmosphere and feelings of fear as there should not be noises.
unwilling baize-covered door	Personification; the door doesn't want to open – suggests something bad inside. Creates atmosphere of foreboding.

(d) (ii)

Choice	Explanation
huge shadowy room	Visual appeal – sense of size and lack of light creates a sense of fear, as without light he is vulnerable.
black window bays / recesses and alcoves / black corners	Visual appeal – sense of lack of light creates a sense of fear as without light he is vulnerable. Also bays suggest hiding places – tension; what is in there?
dusty brown-red hangings	Visual appeal – also atmosphere as red has connotations with blood and evil/danger so creates atmosphere of foreboding.
germinating darknesses	Visual appeal.
candle was a little tongue of light	Personification – visual appeal – light is small and weak. Creates sense of fear as without light he is vulnerable.

vastness of the chamber	Visual appeal – large size – atmosphere – he is vulnerable – he is small within the room – things could be hidden.
an ocean of dull red mystery and suggestion	Metaphor creates visual appeal – idea of the size of the room. Red has connotations with blood and evil / danger so creates atmosphere of foreboding.
sentinel shadows and watching darknesses	Personification and visual appeal sense of foreboding created by idea of being watched.
stillness of desolation brooded over it all.	Personification creates atmosphere: sense of foreboding created by 'brooding'.

Look at the mark scheme below, decide which comments are closest to your answer and then decide what mark to give yourself. This task is marked out of 15 for Reading.

Marks	Comments
13–15	You explain a wide range of effective words. You have discussed meaning and associations of words and their effect, including imagery, precisely. Your answer is balanced so that both halves of it are covered in a consistent manner / quality.
10–12	You explain a well selected collection of words. You explain imagery well. You explain the effect of language in both halves of the question.
7–9	You explain an appropriate group of words. You explain the meanings of words. You discuss effects but in a general way. Your answer is uneven with one half longer / better than the other.
4–6	Some of the words you explain are appropriate but you might have chosen long quotes or ones that are not effective. You do not always explain meanings or you reuse the words in the quotation whilst trying to explain them. You do not always explain effect.
1–3	The words that you have chosen are not relevant/effective. Your comments do not explain how they are effective. You do not explain what effect is created.
0	Your answer does not relate to the question; you may have chosen irrelevant words or no words at all.

4. Writing questions

Gathering information

Skills builder 3

There are many possible sub-headings you could use. Here is a set of sub-headings that might work:
Impressions / Reasons / Hopes.

Skills builder 4

There are many possible groupings of notes you could use. Here are a few examples:

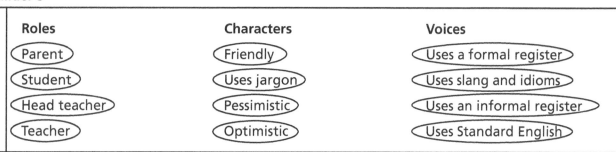

Sub-headings	Notes	Detail
Impressions	Greta is happy Lots of helpers Good support staff / students	'wonderful school' 'teaching assistants' Mr Curtis explained
Reasons	Help struggling child Help students who lack confidence	Greta has had lots of help (red / green cards) Do assemblies
Hopes	My child will develop	Join clubs Make friends

Creating a role using voice and character

Skills builder 5

Roles	Characters	Voices
Parent	Friendly	Uses a formal register
Student	Uses jargon	Uses slang and idioms
Head teacher	Pessimistic	Uses an informal register
Teacher	Optimistic	Uses Standard English

Skills builder 6

There are different aspects of the parents' thoughts and feelings that you could think about, for example:

Head:
My child will do well here.
I hope places are available.

Heart:
She's a sweet girl.
I feel anxious about my child getting a place.

Skills builder 7

1		a)	
2		b)	
3		c)	
4		d)	

Exam-style practice questions: Extended response questions

Mark scheme for extended response question: Reading

Look at the mark scheme below, decide which comments are closest to your answer and then decide what mark to give yourself. This task is marked out of 15 for Reading and out of 10 for Writing.

Marks	Comments
13–15	You have used and developed several ideas (both factual about the school and what happens there and ones that you have inferred about what a prospective student might learn and how they might develop) from the passage. Your answer reflects the feelings of the diary writer consistently and shows that you understand what she thinks about the school and what it could do for her.
10–12	You have used several details about the school and what happens there from the passage. Your answer shows some awareness of the feelings of the diary writer and shows that you understand some of what she thinks about the planned school and what it could do for her.
7–9	You repeat some details about the school and what happens there from the passage. Your answer shows an incomplete understanding of the feelings and thoughts of the diary writer. You have focused on the passage and the question but use the material simply or partially.
4–6	You have written an answer which is relevant to the question, but you tend to retell the passage rather than focus on the three bullet points. You make simple references to the school but they are not 'used' to cover the focus of the question.
1–3	You have tried to use the passage. You retell the passage or give occasional relevant details about the school and the diary writer's reasons for wanting to go there. You may have misunderstood some information or explain in a muddled way.
0	You have not answered the question relevantly or have copied rather than used the passage.

4. Writing questions

Mark scheme for extended response question: Writing

	Marks	Comments
	9–10	You have organised the overall structure of your answer well and your sentences also build up each part in an organised way. You have written in fluent sentences and have used a range of vocabulary. You have used the correct voice for the character of a teenage diary writer.
	7–8	You have organised the overall structure of your answer soundly. You have written in complete sentences (although some may be simple) and have used correct vocabulary. You have sometimes used the correct voice for the character of a teenage diary writer.
	5–6	The overall structure of your diary entry is reasonable and meaning is clear although your sentences are simple and the words you have chosen are basic. You have not written consistently in the correct voice for a teenage diary entry.
	3–4	Your work is not clearly organised and is very simple and not always easy to understand. You may have used too many ideas that have been copied out from the passage.
	1–2	Your diary entry is hard to understand with lots of copying or irrelevant ideas.
	0	Your work cannot be understood.

5. Directed writing questions

Understanding directed writing questions

Skills builder 1

Look at the guidance given for Skills builder 1 of Chapter 4 (page 39) – it provides a useful way to approach making up a mnemonic. Use this table format to create a mnemonic you will find easy to remember.

Gathering and synthesising information

Skills builder 2

The letter could be structured under the following sub-headings: Beliefs and strategies / Opinions / Objections and fears

Skills builder 3

Sub-heading	Point	Detail
Beliefs and strategies	Children pre-conditioned by décor / clothes Children's career choices influenced by time spent on activities as child	Ribbons Dull-coloured clothes for boys Superhero t-shirts Building go-karts Playing in woods
Opinions	Cheaper to have similar rooms / clothes It means wages will become more equal as jobs will not be exclusively male or female	Older son can pass clothes to younger sister Statistics show that wages in exclusively male jobs are higher than in exclusively female jobs
Objections and fears	They will say it is not true	Cousin Jane who became a mechanic

Creating a role using voice and character

Skills builder 4

Roles	Characters	Voices
Child psychologist	Professional	Uses a formal register Uses Standard English
Local nursery owner	Friendly but detached	Uses jargon Uses a formal register
Parent	Anxious to do the best for child	Uses slang and idioms Uses an informal register

Skills builder 5

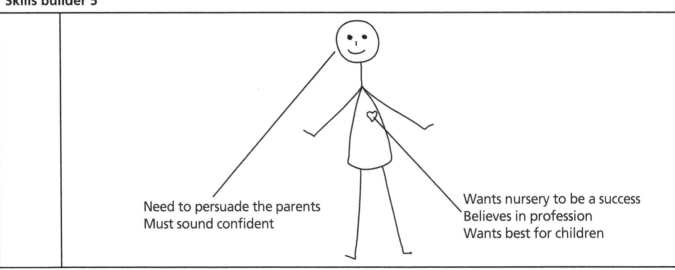

Need to persuade the parents
Must sound confident

Wants nursery to be a success
Believes in profession
Wants best for children

5. Directed writing questions

Skills builder 6

1		a)	
2		b)	
3		c)	
4		d)	

Exam-style practice questions: Directed writing question

Look at the mark schemes below, decide which comments are closest to your answer and then decide what marks to give yourself.

Reading

Marks	Comments
13–15	Your answer shows that you have read the passage about gender thoroughly. You have evaluated lots of ideas (covering all three of the bullets) and have developed them well. You have consistently used details from the passage, which gives a strong sense of direction to your letter.
10–12	Your answer shows that you have read the passage well. You have evaluated a range of ideas about how to bring up their baby and have developed some of them and given some detail such as advice about toys/clothes. All of the bullets are covered.
7–9	You have read the passage quite well but your answer tends to focus on factual details about toy types or jobs and may not cover a wide range of implied ideas from the text. You use some details but do not always utilise them to make a point about how to bring up their baby. Your answer may be unbalanced, focusing on one or two bullets more than others.
5–6	Your answer may give some general understanding of the passage but may lack focus on the bullets or even miss one of them out. You make brief references to material in the text.
3–4	You have understood some of the main ideas in the passage about gender but haven't used it to answer the bullets given, or have given a very general set of answers without much evaluation, detail or development and perhaps some copying out.
0	Your answer doesn't answer the question or perhaps doesn't refer to the passage. You have copied a lot out.

5. Directed writing questions

Writing

Marks	Comments
22–25	It is clear throughout your answer that you are writing to friends who are expecting a baby. You have created a confident and convincing voice as their friend who is concerned and wants to be helpful. Your letter is organised and structured to get your message across effectively. You write fluently and with a wide vocabulary and a wide variety of sentences. Your spelling, punctuation and grammar are always accurate.
18–21	It is almost always clear throughout your answer that you are writing to friends who are expecting a baby. You have clearly tried to create a confident and convincing voice as their friend who is concerned and wants to be helpful. Your letter is mostly organised and structured to get your message across effectively You sometimes write fluently and with a good vocabulary and some variety of sentences. Your spelling, punctuation and grammar are usually accurate.
14–17	Sometimes it is clear that you are writing to friends who are expecting a baby. Your letter shows some organisation and structure, which helps to get your message across effectively. You write clearly, with plain vocabulary and sentences. Your spelling, punctuation and grammar are sound but there are some mistakes.
10–13	Your answer is patchy – at times your audience is clear and at times it is clear that you are grouping information to try to convince your friends but your voice is not always consistent. There are frequent errors in your work.
6–9	Your answer is not clearly expressed and sentences do not flow fluently together to build an argument. There are persistent errors in sentence structure, spelling and grammar, which sometimes make your letter hard to follow.
1–5	Your letter cannot be understood.

6. Composition questions – description

What is descriptive writing?

Skills builder 1

Text C could be a piece of exam-style descriptive writing because text A is asking for a donation and text B is telling as story. Text C is the only text that simply says what is there.

Skills builder 2

- We were hurtling towards the wall like a comet through the sky.
  This text helps us to imagine speed and their height.
- The baby beamed; its cheeks were like rosy apples.
  This text helps us to imagine the shape and colour of the baby's cheeks.

6. Composition questions – description

Skills builder 3

The house smelt dank and musty (5) as I pushed open the door. Spread across the scratched (1/3) oak table, the remains of an evening meal (1), now days old, seemed covered in a white fur blanket. (1) Peaks of muddy gravy-clad potato pierced it here and there, and the vivid green of once freshly picked peas was dulled under a blue-grey haze. Aware of a scrabbling noise, (2) I stumbled awkwardly backwards (1) and watched as tiny mice fled from the nest of shredded paper napkins they had constructed in the shadow of the tarnished old teapot. (1)

(1)	see
(2)	hear
(3)	touch
(4)	taste (although food is featured in the piece we are not encouraged to imagine how it tastes)
(5)	feel

Developing descriptive writing

Skills builder 4

Many different answers are possible. Here is one alternative way of structuring just one of the four descriptions.

As the hurricane hit I saw metal spew from the building in flashing spirals, corkscrew curls of aluminium sheeting as they ripped from the roof and hurtled outwards towards the blackening sky. Seconds later icy shards of window fell to the ground as the windows bowed and broke.

The text above could change to:

As the hurricane hit I stood, transfixed outside the barn and saw metal spew from the building ahead of me in flashing spirals, corkscrew curls of aluminium sheeting across the farmyard as they ripped upward from the roof and hurtled outwards towards the blackening sky. Behind me, icy shards of window fell to the ground as the windows bowed and broke.

Note that the references to time have been replaced by references to place and position.

Skills builder 5

		Add an adjective / adverb	Add an example of figurative language occasionally
	Add how she looks	Her grey hair was blowing in fine wisps around her head.	
	Add what she was doing	As she clenched the battered, weathered tin, which held hundreds of tightly wadded five pound notes, into her apron.	As if they were a dearly loved child.
	Add how she moves	Suddenly she threw her left arm upward and a fountain of notes began to shoot through the sky.	Like papery firework sparks.

Add how things 'feel' to the touch	Occasionally falling back onto her shoulders like gentle feathers.	
Add the sounds that she makes	She laughed out loud, her voice echoing around the headland as the wind carried the notes away over the sea.	Like leaves on an autumn breeze.
Add the smells that come with it		
(Add any tastes if relevant)		

Using imagery and sensory detail in a description

Skills builder 6

- Write a description of a celebration – relieved and positive
- Waiting at the dentist – tense and scared
- The party – happy and positive
- The castle – dark and foreboding
- A typical villain – negative and frightening

Skills builder 7

Many answers are possible. Here is a possible answer to **b)**: if the dancer was playing a character who shared those characteristics – perhaps a sly, shifty character who moves furtively without people noticing.

Skills builder 8

There are many possible answers. Here are some suggestions to get your imagination working:
- You might use words to describe the workers as: worker bees, queen bee, drones, colony, nurse bee, scout.
- You might describe individuals using words such as: antennae, barb, mandibles.
- You might describe objects using words such as: wax, honey, pollen.
- You might describe the office environment using words such as: hive, crowded, busy.

Exam-style practice questions: Composition questions – description

Composition: content and structure

Marks	General criteria	Specific criteria
14–15	**Content:** Your choices of description are clever and purposeful and build an overall impression. **Structure:** Your description has a clear, secure and balanced structure to guide the reader through it.	Your description creates an overall picture and a sense of focus on a variety of focal points. Many individual features are well described and brought to life.
11–13	**Content:** You develop some interesting and relevant descriptions. **Structure:** Your writing is orderly and has a good start and finish.	Your description does not create a consistent overall picture but it focuses on specifics to paint realistic elements.
8–10	**Content:** You describe objects and individuals with some detail. **Structure:** Some of your writing creates well structured sequences where the details fit together.	You describe a selection of focal points well but may link them together via a narrative.
5–7	**Content:** You describe relevant things and give a little detail. **Structure:** You create a pathway through the description but parts of it are unbalanced and you may focus too long on one thing.	You write about a series of details but they are not selected so that they create an effect on the reader, and they tend to build a narrative not a description.
3–4	**Content:** Your description may not be believable, or may only be believable occasionally. **Structure:** Some of your paragraphing is insecure and some sentences do not link together well.	The emphasis of your writing is on narrative rather than descriptive detail.
1–2	**Content:** Some of your descriptions are useful to the reader but others are unclear or irrelevant. **Structure:** Your work is muddled and there isn't a clear pathway through the description that can be followed.	Your writing does not include enough detail to create effective description.
0	**Content:** The things that you describe do not help the reader to gain a sense of place or people and you do not write enough. **Structure:** Your work doesn't seem to have a structure at all.	There is no sense of a cohesive description building up.

Composition: style and accuracy

Marks	Comments
21–25	Your writing shows a consistent sense for audience through word choices and sentence structures, which are obviously used for effect. Your spelling, punctuation and grammar are almost always accurate.
17–20	Your writing is beginning to show evidence of crafting to suit your audience and to create effects. It is mainly accurate and words and sentences are clearly chosen for their effect at times.
13–16	Your writing achieves its purpose but without flair; it is simply written with occasionally adventurous word choices and sentence structures. Small but regular errors of spelling, punctuation and grammar.
9–12	Your writing is easy to understand and is effective at times but this is not consistent and at other times there is a lack of range of sentences and vocabulary and errors in spelling, punctuation and grammar.
5–8	Your writing is simple but it is possible to understand what you mean most of the time. There are lots of errors in your sentence structure, spelling, punctuation and grammar.
1–4	Your writing is weak and it is often hard to understand what you mean. Your sentences are often long and rambling or punctuated incorrectly. There are many mistakes in your spelling and grammar.
0	It is not possible to read your work. Your sentences, spelling punctuation and grammar are all inaccurate, which makes the meaning unclear.

What is narrative writing?

Skills builder 1

Text A represents a piece of exam-style narrative writing because it introduces characters, a setting and a potential story arc.

Skills builder 2

The notes could be arranged in the following ways.

The Disaster	The Meeting
Setting: Rainy day in a small city apartment in Paris.	Setting: Hot summer in large rambling country house in Wales.
Characters: Elderly resident, grandson, 17. Workmen re-roofing older part of apartment.	Characters: Girl, 18, and her mother, who is a single parent.
Narrator: First person, male	Narrator: First person, female
Grandson calls to see elderly grandmother and offers to make her a drink.	A girl receives a letter from a girl who says she is her twin.
Workman is working on roofing but falls off ladder to ground and is hurt but nobody can see / hear him.	She searches her mum's drawers and finds a birth certificate.
Blowtorch being used on roof sets the timbers alight.	She asks her mother about it but her mother gets angry and walks out.
Grandson smells smoke when talking to grandmother and rushes out to alert workman.	Her mum comes back and sees the birth certificate so they talk about what happened.
Grandson finds workman, who has injured his leg. Calls ambulance.	Girl is shocked and upset but realises her mother had to make a difficult choice and accepts this.
Grandson climbs onto roof to put out fire.	They go together to meet the twin.
Grandson stumbles and gets foot caught in roofing. Struggles but gets free.	
Grandson returns to grandmother who wants more tea.	

7. Composition questions – narrative

How is narrative writing structured?

Skills builder 3

Use a story you know well and split it into five narrative parts, e.g. a version of Little Red Riding Hood.

1.	Introduction: A little girl lives in a house in the woods with her father, who is a woodcutter. Her grandmother lives in the woods and so does a wolf.
2.	Rising action: The girl goes to visit her grandmother but she strays off the path.
3.	Climax: The wolf eats the girl and her grandmother.
4.	Falling action: The girl's father attacks the wolf and cuts it open.
5.	Resolution: The girl and her grandmother escape from the wolf's belly.

Skills builder 4

There are many ways of adding detail. Possible details might include the following:
Igor wearily looked up from the towering pile of letters and ledgers covering his dusty desk and brushed his tangled hair out of his tired eyes.

There are many ways of adding dialogue. Possible dialogue might include the following:
'What do you mean? What are you talking about? I haven't been hiding anything … much.'

Creating character and setting

Skills builder 5

The table below lists some possible examples of what can be inferred from the details we have been given. Try to come up with more inferrences.

Detail	What we can infer
… said Marion, no mean cook herself in her own estimation	She has a high opinion of herself.
She had brought a Bakewell tart with her as a gift	She is polite / trying to impress?
So it was Irene now. Last time she was here they had still been on 'Mrs Litton' terms.	Marion is becoming more familiar with Irene.
Marion's hair was redder and darker than it had been at the beginning of the week and her little marmoset face more brightly painted.	Marion is trying hard to look good when she visits the house; she wants to impress.
She couldn't sit still for five minutes but was up and down, bouncing about on her little stick legs and her kitten heels.	She is restless / anxious.
… she had served and cleared away the coffee	She is making herself useful / feels at home / is trying to impress.

7. Composition questions – narrative

Skills builder 6

The table below lists some of the things the text shows us about Marion and Mrs Litton.

Dialogue	What this shows about Marion / Mrs Litton
'Absolutely delicious, Irene'	Marion is trying to flatter Mrs Litton.
'If I shut my eyes I might be in Bologna.'	Marion has travelled / is educated / is trying to impress.
'You mustn't think you have to come with me,'	Marion is trying to provoke him / putting words into his mouth?
'It's no trouble,'	His mother wants him to take Marion home / wants them to get together.

Exam-style practice questions: Composition question – narrative

Composition: Content and Structure

Marks	General criteria	Specific criteria
14–15	**Content:** Your choices of description are clever and purposeful and build an overall impression. **Structure:** Your description has a clear, secure and balanced structure to guide the reader through it.	Your story is structured so that it builds towards or away from a key moment. You use description and dialogue to create characters and settings.
11–13	**Content:** You develop some interesting and relevant descriptions. **Structure:** Your writing is orderly and has a good start and finish.	Your story uses elements of a good story but not consistently; so there may be an over-long build up or ending, or too much narrative or description at times.
8–10	**Content:** You describe objects and individuals with some detail. **Structure:** Some of your writing creates well structured sequences where the details fit together.	You have written a straightforward story with some details such as dialogue or description of character and place.

	5–7	**Content:** You describe relevant things and give a little detail. **Structure:** You create a pathway through the description but parts of it are unbalanced and you may focus too long on one thing.	Your story is probably a little unrealistic or severely unbalanced so that you spend far too long on one stage of it. You may not have very much, or far too much, dialogue or description so that at times the reader forgets that it is a story.
	3–4	**Content:** Your description may not be believable, or may only be believable occasionally. **Structure:** Some of your paragraphing is insecure and some sentences do not link together well.	Some of your story is unrealistic and it may be hard to understand at times.
	1–2	**Content:** Some of your descriptions are useful to the reader but others are unclear or irrelevant. **Structure:** Your work is muddled and there isn't a clear pathway through the description that can be followed.	It is not clear what is important or significant in your story and at times it is not clear.
	0	**Content:** The things you describe do not help the reader to gain a sense of place or people and you do not write enough. **Structure:** Your work doesn't seem to have a structure at all.	Your story is not really relevant or is very hard to follow.

7. Composition questions – narrative

Composition: style and accuracy

Marks	Comments
21–25	Your writing shows a consistent sense for audience through word choices and sentence structures, which are obviously used for effect. Your spelling, punctuation and grammar are almost always accurate.
17–20	Your writing is beginning to show evidence of crafting to suit your audience and to create effects. It is mainly accurate and words and sentences are clearly chosen for their effect at times.
13–16	Your writing achieves its purpose but without flair; it is simply written with occasionally adventurous word choices and sentence structures. Small but regular errors of spelling, punctuation and grammar.
9–12	Your writing is easy to understand and is effective at times but this is not consistent and at other times there is a lack of range of sentences and vocabulary and errors in spelling, punctuation and grammar.
5–8	Your writing is simple but it is possible to understand what you mean most of the time. There are lots of errors in your sentence structure, spelling, punctuation and grammar.
1–4	Your writing is weak and it is often hard to understand what you mean. Your sentences are often long and rambling or punctuated incorrectly. There are many mistakes in your spelling and grammar.
0	It is not possible to read your work. Your sentences, spelling punctuation and grammar are all inaccurate, which makes the meaning unclear.

Glossary

Section 1: Reading 1 – Comprehension Questions	
Factual	something known to be true.
Inference	an idea gleaned by reading between the lines, or using clues in language to work out a meaning.

Section 1: Reading 4 – Extended response to reading Section 2: Direct Writing and Composition 5 – Directed writing questions	
Character	a person's personality, values and beliefs.
Idioms	typical phrases common to a language.
Jargon	a type of language relating to a particular job or role.
Register	a level of address, e.g. formal / informal.
Role	the part someone is playing or a category they fit into.
Standard English	language use which adheres to recognised grammatical rules and uses no abbreviations, slang or idioms.
Voice	the personal expression and language an individual uses.

Section 1: Reading 2 – Summary writing questions	
Implicit	a meaning that is not based on a dictionary definition but relies upon associations or connotations being added to the word.
Literal	a meaning that relies on the dictionary definition of a word and involves no inference.
Main ideas	key ideas, without which a text would not make sense.
Paraphrasing	re-wording an original piece of text.
Scan	to read, looking for specific word types or features, or specific pieces of information.
Synonyms	words which mean the same.

Section 1: Reading 3 – Short answer and language questions	
Emotive language	words which create an emotional response.
Engage	to draw someone in by interesting or stimulating them.
Figurative language	using figures of speech such as similes and metaphors to create effect.
Imagery	words or comparisons that create a mental picture.
Implicit	a meaning that is not based on a dictionary definition but relies upon associations or connotations being added to the word.
Metaphors	a vivid comparison that does not use 'as' or 'like'.
Sensory picture	a description which stimulates the reader's senses and allows them to imagine that they are 'there'.
Similes	a vivid comparison of two things or ideas using 'like' or 'as'.
Section 2: Directed Writing and Composition 6 – Composition questions – description	
Adjectives	a word that describes a noun.
Adverbs	a word that describes a verb.
Figurative language	using figures of speech such as similes and metaphors to create effect.
Semantic field	a set of words that refer to a subject and are grouped by meaning.
Structured	to have an order or hierarchy.